TOWARD INDEPENDENCE

Henri Cartier-Bresson

*Painting of a Dutch Governor
being carried out of the Batavia palace before celebrations
for the newly recognized Republic of Indonesia,
December 31, 1949.*

Edited by Jane Levy Reed

TOWARD INDEPENDENCE

A Century of Indonesia Photographed

THE FRIENDS OF PHOTOGRAPHY, SAN FRANCISCO

This publication is made possible through the support of:

The Columbia Foundation

Rosewood Stone Group

Springhouse Foundation

Thendara Foundation

Wee Bee Bop

Published in conjunction with an exhibition organized
by The Friends of Photography and presented at the Ansel Adams Center in San Francisco,
September 25–December 1, 1991.

ISBN 0-933286-58-9
Library of Congress Catalogue No. 91-71572

CREDITS

Permission to reproduce the photographs included in this book has been granted by the following
individuals and institutions and is gratefully acknowledged:

Mrs. Elanore Adam, New York City, pages 90, 91, 93–95;

Leo Haks Rare Books, Amsterdam, pages 17, 28, 34, 49, 56, 57, 58,61, 70, 71, 83, 86, 92;

The Kern Institute, Leiden, the Netherlands, pages 36, 40–44, 51, 52;

Magnum Photos, Inc., Paris, pages 8, 31, 48, 55, 60, 64, 68, 69;

The Menil Collection, Houston, pages 109, 110;

Museum of Ethnology, Rotterdam, pages 31–33, 35, 50, 62, 63, 72, 76–78, 82, 118;

The Netherlands Study and Documentation Centre for Photography,

Leiden University, the Netherlands, pages 20, 24, 26, 27;

Tropenmuseum, Amsterdam, pages 8, 48, 55, 60, 64, 68, 69, 84, 85, 116;

and the Walter Spies Foundation, Leiden, pages 96, 100–105.

Edited by Jane Levy Reed
Production coordinated by David Featherstone
Designed by Adelaida Mejia Design
Set in Adobe Garamond, Adobe Garamond Expert and Futura
Printing and Duotones by Phelps Schaefer Lithographics Inc.
Bound by Pacific Trade Bindery

THE FRIENDS OF PHOTOGRAPHY

The Friends of Photography, founded in 1967 in Carmel, California,
is a privately funded, member–supported organization housed
in the Ansel Adams Center in San Francisco.
The programs of The Friends in publications, exhibitions, education and awards to photographers
are guided by a commitment to photography as a fine art and to the discussion
of photographic ideas through critical inquiry.
The publications of The Friends emphasize contemporary photography
yet are also concerned with the criticism and history of the medium.
They include the newsletter re:view, the book series Untitled and major photographic monographs.
Membership is open to everyone. To receive an informational membership brochure
and a list of available publications, write to
The Friends of Photography, Ansel Adams Center,
250 Fourth Street, San Francisco, California 94103.
The Friends receives major support from the California Arts Council
and the National Endowment for the Arts.

CONTENTS

CONTRIBUTORS

JOHN BLOOM is a San Francisco–based photographer, curator, critic and educator who has written extensively about a variety of subjects in photography. He has been instrumental in organizing the exhibition and publication *Toward Independence*.

ERIC CRYSTAL is an anthropologist and coordinator of Southeast Asian studies at the University of California, Berkeley. He has done extensive field work in the outer islands of Indonesia, publishing in film, video and audio recording.

JAN FONTEIN is director emeritus of the Asian Art Collection of the Boston Museum of Fine Arts. He is an acknowledged expert in Borobudur, and is curator of the Festival of Indonesia exhibition *Sculpture of Indonesia*.

ANNEKE GROENEVELD is curator of the iconographical collection at the Museum of Ethnology in Rotterdam, the Netherlands. She has authored or edited a number of photography publications for the museum.

KUNANG HELMI is an Indonesian writer and photographer who lives in Paris. Her interests include textiles, arts and crafts, design, photography and film. She has edited several books on Indonesia.

HEDI HINZLER is professor of Southeast Asian Studies at the Leiden University, the Netherlands. She has written numerous books and articles on Indonesia and is president of the Walter Spies Foundation.

PETER KORS was born in Bandung, West Java, of Dutch–Indonesian colonial ancestry. An actor and a singer/songwriter, he specializes in telling stories from Indonesia and other cultures around the world.

H. J. MOESHART is assistant curator of the Study and Documentation Centre for Photography at Leiden University. He is particularly interested in Japanese photography from 1850 to 1875.

JANE LEVY REED, editor of *Toward Independence*, is a photographer, independent curator and Indonesian scholar who, since 1974, has lived and frequently traveled in Indonesia and other parts of Southeast Asia.

PAULINE LUNSINGH SCHEURLEER is head of the Department of Asiatic Art of the Rijksmuseum in Amsterdam, and curator of art of South and Southeast Asia. Her primary area of research is sculpture of the classical Indonesian period.

YUDHI SOERJOATMODJO is a photographer and chief photo–editor at *TEMPO* Magazine, Indonesia's premier newsweekly. He studied economics and photography in Paris and has written many articles on photography in modern Indonesia.

JOHN STOWELL is senior lecturer in German at the University of Newcastle, New South Wales, Australia. He is writing an extensive critical biography of Walter Spies and editing a volume of Spies' correspondence.

ADRIAN VICKERS is a lecturer in Southeast Asian History at the University of Wollongong, Australia. He has done extensive research on Balinese history, art and literature as well as on Western images of Bali.

ACKNOWLEDGEMENTS

One late night in Bali, the idea for this exhibition and publication was conceived while walking down a dusty road with my dear friend Alan Feinstein, director of programs for the arts for the Ford Foundation in Jakarta, Indonesia. In discussing the Festival of Indonesia, then in the planning stages, and its extensive list of exhibitions, we both realized that none would be photographic. Alan felt that my background in photography and my knowledge of the country made a perfect marriage of abilities to create a photographic component for the Festival. My journey began, and two years later, with the help of numerous supporters, *Toward Independence: A Century of Indonesia Photographed* has come to fruition.

The Festival of Indonesia Committee in both New York and Indonesia accepted the idea, and they have been extremely supportive of the project. I extend my appreciation to the organizers of the Festival—Ted Tanen, Anthony Granucci, Maggie Weintraub, Niki Phillips and Cecelia Levin. Thomas Seligman, of the M. H. de Young Museum, Fine Arts Museums of San Francisco, was instrumental in introducing the project to Ronald Egherman, executive director of The Friends of Photography. Ron enthusiastically embraced the idea of producing the exhibition for the Ansel Adams Center and publishing this catalogue. Sincere appreciation is extended to both of them, as well as to the staff of The Friends.

After researching many collections, from the Claire Holt Collection at the Lincoln Center Archives in New York City to the Colin McPhee Collection at the University of California, Los Angeles, Dr. Hildred Geertz, of Princeton University, told me, "Go to the Netherlands, my friend; it's all there." It made sense, of course, since Holland had been Indonesia's colonial ruler for three hundred years, important materials would surely be archived there.

There are many people behind the scenes whose guidance, professional skills and friendship have greatly contributed to this project. They include Sandra Phillips, Diana du Pont, Eric Crystal, Edward Guerrero and Bruce Katz. Kunang Helmi was pivotal in helping my research both in the United States and abroad; her fundraising efforts are also appreciated. My meetings with M. Henri Cartier–Bresson were a wonderful source of shared feelings, insight and inspiration; and Tassilo Adam's daughter–in–law, Mrs. Elanore Adam, was most generous with her time as well as with her photographic collection.

Sincere appreciation is due to the book's writers for the depth of their research and the breadth of their contributions. They have certainly broken new critical ground in their discussions of Indonesian photography. For their gracious generosity and assistance beyond the call of curatorial duty, I am also grateful to Marie–Pierre Giffey, of Magnum Photos, Inc., in Paris; Henk Van Rinsum of the Tropenmuseum in Amsterdam; Anneke Groeneveld, of the Museum of Ethnology in Rotterdam; Pauline Scheurleer of the Rijksmuseum in Amsterdam; Hedi Hinzler, of Leiden University; Leo Haks, of Amsterdam; H. J. Moeshart, of the Prentenkabinet in Leiden; and Ellen Raven, of the Kern Institute in Leiden. Thanks also to Jan van de Kooi, for his excellent reproduction photographs, and to Adelaida Mejia, for her sensitive design of the book. Sjamsir Sjarif provided Indonesian translations of wall–label material for the exhibition.

For their generosity in helping to fund the exhibition and publication, recognition goes to the Columbia Foundation, the Springhouse Foundation, the Thendara Foundation and Rosewood Stone Group. Special thanks goes to David Featherstone for supervising production of the catalogue and particularly for skillfully meeting the challenge presented by sixteen essays from writers in several different countries. His time and heartfelt interest in both Indonesia and this project have been a tremendous sustaining thread.

Finally, I would like to extend my deepest gratitude to Larry Reed, for his faith in my abilities; and to John Bloom, for his constant help and support, persistent encouragement, insightful curatorial eye and profound friendship. Without him, *Toward Independence* would never have reached completion.

Jane Levy Reed
May 1991

Thilly Weissenborn

Balinese Legong *dancer*
in front of the ornate frame of a gamelan gong,

c. 1920.

Introduction

Jane Levy Reed

FROM ITS VERY INCEPTION, PHOTOGRAPHY HAS BEEN AN INVALUABLE TOOL FOR REPRESENTING AND UNDERSTANDING THE WORLD'S DIVERSE AND COMPLEX CULTURES. IN THE MID–NINETEENTH CENTURY, THE ADVENTURESOME PHOTOGRAPHER HAD TO TAKE A WAGON LOAD OF EQUIPMENT INTO THE FIELD AND MIGHT HAVE SPENT AN ENTIRE DAY MAKING ONE SUCCESSFUL PHOTOGRAPH. TODAY, THROUGH ONGOING TECHNOLOGICAL ADVANCES, that wagon has been reduced to a backpack, and the contemporary photographer is likely to take hundreds of exposures for each one he or she ultimately uses. In the century–and–a–half of photography's aesthetic and technological development, photographers have directed their lenses at every facet of the world, and their photographs range from intimate family portraits and sweeping historical panoramas to illuminating ethnographic details hidden in the lives of remote indigenous peoples. In the process, this enormous enterprise has created a worldwide visual language that has augmented our historical memory. Photography has reconfigured our aesthetic perceptions and has brought the planet's diverse societies together through a perpetually circulating matrix of photographic images, signs and icons.

Toward Independence: A Century of Indonesia Photographed chronicles the development of this kind of matrix—a significant one–hundred–year era within the longer transformation of Indonesia, from its colonial occupation by the Dutch, which began in the 1500s, to its emergence as an independent nation in 1945. It is hoped that this collection of work by twelve photographers will convey and symbolize the strength and spirit of the Indonesian people and inspire us all to become more deeply aware of the complex social and cultural issues facing them today. Although the collection features photographers whose work spans ten decades, it tries to avoid a fixed sense of periodization while at the same time it recognizes the subtle ambience of historical narrative that permeates many of these images. This book and the exhibition that it accompanies reveal the broad range of perspectives that have contributed to the evolution of Indonesia's dynamic, diversified visual culture.

The Indonesian archipelago is a vast yet heterogeneous complex of islands, languages, cultures and religions, with Hinduism, Buddhism, Animism, Islam and Christianity coexisting in a bewildering variety of expressions and overlays. Moreover, the nation's social structures are inextricably bound to religious beliefs and practices, a milieu unfamiliar to modern, secular, Western sensibilities. These religions and belief systems create a delicate and dynamic web of social forms, customs and tensions that is constantly mediated by the nation's people in their aesthetic and intellectual endeavors as well as in their daily lives.

No single photographic exhibition, no matter how ambitious, could hope to present a complete historical picture of Indonesia's enormous cultural richness and diversity. In determining the conceptual focus for *Toward Independence,* hundreds of daguerreotypes and photographs of Indonesia were reviewed, from collections both in the United States and in Europe. Of the several thousand images considered, some of the finest were found in forgotten country attics, family albums and dusty Dutch drawers. Still others came perfectly preserved from metropolitan archives. As the selection process progressed, patterns gradually emerged and ideas began to crystallize. While the majority of the photographs viewed commanded interest from an historical, anthropological or ethnographic point of view, many of them sorely lacked the compositional and aesthetic qualities of overpowering, memorable images.

To be included, each photograph had to be powerful enough to address the viewer on its own merits, perhaps as a unique articulation of its historical moment or as an icon alluding to the splendors of Indonesia's pre-colonial and colonial past. Images were selected that would convey some deeper essence of Indonesia that was ambient and persistent in spite of the thin overlay of colonialism. Most important though, each photograph had to have something of that often ambiguous, compelling quality that captures the spectator's imagination. Correspondingly, a photographer was chosen from each decade who was best able to render the country's considerable visual beauty and cultural diversity and to enhance our understanding of that period of time.

While the majority of these pre-Independence image-makers were European born and came to Indonesia out of their own commercial interests, or on commission in the service of some colonial enterprise, *Toward Independence* is graced by one of the first indigenous Indonesian photographers as well as one of the first women to photograph in colonial Asia. Each photographer was ultimately selected for his or her aesthetic vision. Some of them were trained as painters, while others took up photography as businessmen or hobbyists. They came from such varied places as Armenia, the Netherlands, Germany, England, the United States and Indonesia itself. While some fell under the spell of the archipelago's exotic charm, others found inspiration in the ordinary moments of cultural expression played out in practices of everyday life. All, however, developed a deep sense of place and devotion to the magic, mystery and interplay of human and cultural forces that they came to know in Indonesia.

The earliest photographer in the collection is Adolph Schaefer, who studied with Daguerre in France and quickly recognized the daguerreotype's potential to bring the most remote corners of the world into the living rooms of the rising, industrial European nations. In the 1840s, Schaefer had the opportunity to do some of his finest work when he convinced the Dutch government to commission him to photograph monuments and landscapes in what was then the Dutch East Indies.

The adventurers Walter Bentley Woodbury and James Page owned a commercial photography house that dealt in views, postcards and stock pictures. In the process of gathering picturesque images, they traveled the globe and spent an extensive period of time in Indonesia. Their aesthetic sense was expressed in a stylized topographic vision of the world and in vignetted portraits of Indonesian and Dutch royalty.

Isidore Van Kinsbergen was formally trained as an artist and was retained as a photographer for the Batavian Society of Arts and Sciences. He is best known for a creative manipulation of light that evoked a sense of mythic imagery residing in the statues and architecture he photographed. This ability to render form as myth and metaphor lends a dramatic touch to Van Kinsbergen's precise descriptions.

Van Kinsbergen is followed by the pioneer Indonesian photographer Kassian Céphas, who worked extensively at the grand Buddhist temple complex of Borobudur and is best known for his work in the *keratons*, the royal palaces of Yogyakarta and Solo. One of the first photographers to be employed by and admitted to the sequestered world of the royal courts, his portraits of Javanese courtiers, dignitaries and royal dancers brought an indigenous Indonesian sensibility to what was then a European–dominated medium.

In almost total contrast to these tendencies of pictorialism and aestheticism, the photographer Charles J. Kleingrothe, working in the 1880s, surveyed Indonesia's emerging commercial culture. He documented tobacco plantations, factories and warehouses peopled with indigenous laborers and Chinese field hands, and his pictures make us aware of the role of class, race and labor in the mercantile economy.

By the final decade of the nineteenth century, the photographic process had become cheaper and more convenient, and photography had begun to establish itself as a vastly popular medium and as a means of making a professional living. This resulted in a flurry of photographic activity throughout the world, and Indonesia was no exception. In the 1890s, Onnes Kurkdjian, an Armenian with an ornate sensibility, traveled through Indonesia making elaborate still lifes, lavish portraits and pastoral landscapes. One can see the diversity of Kurkdjian's subject matter in photographs that range from the primordial Bromo volcano caught in the act of erupting to the sterile, confined spaces of colonial Dutch waiting rooms and a stiff, royal reception for Queen Wilhelmina. Kurkdjian's motivation was primarily commercial, and he produced volumes of images for sale to foreign and local dignitaries.

One of the most notable photographers also working during this period was C. W. Nieuwenhuis, a painter who received an extensive art education in Germany. Nieuwenhuis brought a painter's sense of construction, perception and grandeur to his photographic landscapes, imbuing them with a richness and intensity often overlooked by those of more commercial predilection. He also demonstrated a disciplined sense of ethnographic detail wrought with a fine aesthetic edge when he made some of the first images of Nias warriors of Sumatra and their elaborate tribal culture. Ultimately, his can be described as an orderly vision marked by painterly imagination and clarity of description that took as its focus works ranging from distant views to genre studies.

Meanwhile, the violent resistance to Dutch domination by the Acehnese in northern Sumatra had begun (1873–1914), and Dr. H. M. Neeb, a Dutch physician and photographer living and working in Indonesia, found himself caught up in the human drama of that conflict. With the detached eye of a clinician, he was able to document the casualties of war and portray the attitudes of its survivors. His stark, provocative images of war dead remind us of the immense cost of empire to indigenous populations as the colonials met resistance to their quest for territory and power.

Thilly Weissenborn, a Dutch woman who learned her craft at Kurkdjian's studio, struck out on her own in the second decade of the twentieth century. She brought a new sensibility to photography with her insightful portraits of Balinese women and dancers, her dramatic landscapes and her fascination with the archipelago's many cultural rituals and religious expressions. Her ability to interact with and feature women as special subjects for her camera was important to the construction of her images. In Weissenborn's portrait of a Balinese dancer, seated in her elaborate costume and framed in the arch of a gong–stand, one can sense her appreciation of the innate dignity and power of young nascent womanhood articulated as a delicate ambiguity registered in the dancer's facial expression and bodily posture.

In the 1920s, Tassilo Adam began working in Indonesia as the official ethnographic photographer for the Netherlands Indies Government. He spent fourteen years living among the Batak people of north Sumatra. So great was his identification with the cultural life of the indigenous people that he renounced Christianity and submerged himself totally in their beliefs and practices. Adam is best known for his films and stills of the dancers and performers in the royal courts of central Java. He imparted a considerable amount of dignity and respect to his subjects because of his commitment and sensitivity to their culture, and his multi–panel panoramas of Java added much to the photographic legacy of Indonesia.

Walter Spies, a well–known German artist living in Indonesia in the 1930s, took dramatic photographs of the performing arts, the practice of everyday life and the archipelago's many cultural rituals. He was a powerful painter, and his photographs echo the shadows and multiple perspectives so finely articulated in his work on canvas. His images of *barong* spirits dancing in the mists of cultural antiquity evoke a haunting sensibility that draws upon the intersection of myth, dream and ceremonial reality. One can feel the universal unconscious in these photographs, the "return of the repressed" dancing in twilight.

Finally, Henri Cartier–Bresson's photographs bring *Toward Independence* to the middle decade of the twentieth century. With the arrival of nationhood for Indonesia, Cartier–Bresson photographed the evacuation of the Dutch, the elevation of the nationalist leaders, the spirit of the independence movement and the explosive drama of the Balinese trance dance. His dynamic vision and his modern instinct for photographing telling moments rather than poses or constructed tableaux is profoundly evident in his Indonesian work.

Viewing the photographs of *Toward Independence* from a contemporary standpoint, one is led to speculate on the parade of meanings that they have held over the years. Surely, adventurers inspired by European expansion and the colonial, orientalist imagination used early photographs to spin stories of fabulous, decadent kingdoms filled with gold and spices. Indonesia certainly evokes thoughts of a stereotypical tropical paradise in even the most casual observer, yet while some westerners found paradise in Indonesia's grand array of cultures and aesthetic expressions, others thought they found it in the beauty and ritual of the royal courts. This was a cruel deception, however, for during the three hundred years of contact with, and then occupation by the Dutch, the real political power of Indonesia's kings and sultans gradually eroded. In response, these courtly figures turned inward, and behind the palace walls they created a world of incredible beauty and perfection, a world of gilded poet kings, elegant courtiers and royal dancers. But it was also a world of intrigue and deception, fixed by colonial relations in a static moment that nostalgically evoked a classical past that was long gone.

Our own perspectives and perceptions of a given photograph shift constantly under the pressure of political and aesthetic hindsight. Thus in Cartier–Bresson's image of Sukarno, the first president of Indonesia and the leader of its independence movement, shown with a determined smile and clenched fists in front of a painting of young freedom fighters who had sacrificed much for their cause, looks different today than it did during the Cold War, or to an Indonesian nationalist. Meaning thus resides both in the photograph and the viewer and is the sum of their interaction. Even those familiar with Indonesian culture will find surprises in the work of the twelve photographers presented here, surprises based on the revelation of unexpected details and the candor of the subjects. The modern audience so accustomed to the plethora of visual images in culture should take the time to challenge the obvious beauty of the subjects of these photographs. *Toward Independence, A Century of Indonesia Photographed* examines this culture in all of its historical complexity.

Imaging Indonesia *Cultural Context and Historic Process*

Eric Crystal

LONG BEFORE GREAT RELIGIONS, AGGRESSIVE MERCHANTS AND COMMITTED IDEOLOGUES BEGAN TO SHAPE MODERN INDONESIA, A HOST OF CULTURES AND COMMUNITIES DEVELOPED REFINED ADAPTATIONS TO THE ISLAND WORLD OF EQUATORIAL SOUTHEAST ASIA. ALMOST WITHOUT EXCEPTION, THE PEOPLES OF THE INDONESIAN ISLANDS SPEAK TONGUES OF A SINGLE LANGUAGE FAMILY (AUSTRONESIAN), SHARE COMMON ENVIRONMENTAL AND SPIRITUAL CONCERNS about rice agriculture and possess elaborate craft and art traditions manifested in architecture, carving and textiles. These cultures became established in seacoast and mangrove coastal areas, successfully farmed deep into the inland rainforest and consistently produced significant surplus rice crops on expansive inland plains that were often fertilized with cyclical showers of volcanic ash. Common themes of culture, subsistence agriculture and language bind the peoples of this vast tropical archipelago together despite the wide dispersion of ethnic groups across thirteen thousand islands.

The cultures of Indonesia developed over many millennia of migration, adaptation and cultural evolution. Throughout the archipelago, island cultures are marked by hoary myths of origin and ancient lore of migration. Many such stories recount ancestors' departures by sailing craft, recall their perilous sea journeys and mark their first landfall and settlement of harbors, valleys and hillsides. In many cases, unusual stones, deep springs and great banyan trees mark the place of first settlement where progenitors—today often elevated to the rank of deities—are thought to have erected the first clan house and farmed the first cultivated field. Such myths of original settlement are frequently enhanced by tales recounting the first planting of sacred seeds from which subsequent crops of rice are thought to have descended. Notions of the goddess of rice, a figure most graphically depicted in a plethora of folk arts, are common throughout the region. These depictions range from abstract designs carved on bamboo offering platforms to living Balinese tapestries fashioned from the supple leaves of the sugar palm to intricate designs incorporated into the *ikat* fabrics of the eastern Indonesian islands.

Ecology, economics and history have combined to create a significant distinction between the core, inner–island regions of Java and Bali and the peripheral, or outer–island regions that cover two–thirds of today's Indonesian national territory. The fertile volcanic soils of Java and adjacent Bali have enabled rice agriculture to flourish, and populations there have expanded. On Java, the influence of traders and religious teachers from India was most pronounced in the 1200s, when contact was first made by Indian traders sailing east through the Java Sea. Monuments standing in the cool mists of the Dieng Plateau, in central Java, attest to this earliest impact of Hinduism. Local rulers validated and enhanced their power by their association with traders and Hindu teachers

Henri Cartier-Bresson

Sumatran rice fields,

1949.

from across the seas. Literacy was acquired, first in Sanskrit and subsequently as a result of centuries of Indian influence. A distinct Javanese script was also developed, one of the many profound consequences of the coming of Hindu civilization.

The subsequent emergence of precolonial kingdoms and trading states on Java and Bali and along coastal Sumatra reinforced the distinction between center and periphery in Indonesia. The impact of great kingdoms such as Mataram and Madjapahit extended not only throughout Java, but overseas to outlying regions as well. Court regalia surviving in locales such as South Sulawesi, eastern Sumatra and southern Kalimantan (Borneo) attest to the degree of commercial intercourse and cultural contact between rulers of the outer–island, non–Javanese kingdoms and the powerful states of the center.

Alphonse de Albuquerque, the indefatigable Portuguese explorer and adventurer who searched in vain across the wilds of northern Mexico for the fabled seven cities of gold, was the first European to make an impact in Southeast Asia. In 1511, Albuquerque's fleet engaged the Sultanate of Malacca on the west coast of the Malay peninsula in a deadly struggle for control of a rich trade in spices and silks. Many of the riches of island Southeast Asia were brought to Malacca, a flourishing Muslim coastal city, sold there and transported either north to the coast of China or west to India, the Levant and ultimately Europe. Albuquerque's defeat of Malacca presaged first the compromise and then the annihilation of independent island states in the region. The intrusion of European forces opened the way for western trading companies to establish alien monopoly control of local economies by force of arms; and, over time, firms such has the Netherlands East Indies Trading Company not only conducted trade, but increasingly governed through an elaborate system of administrative control.

In the sixteenth and seventeenth centuries, Dutch traders dominated and developed their capital of Batavia, on the northwestern coast of Java; but, as Dutch influence spread throughout the island, it was confronted by a powerful and intrinsically hostile counter force, Islam. In the three centuries preceding the arrival of Albuquerque in Southeast Asia, the ideological and moral force of Islam had wrought fundamental changes throughout the region. Islam entered Indonesia by way of coastal India, first making its impact on trading ports of western and northern Sumatra, slowly spreading throughout harbor cities and trading centers. By the mid–fourteenth century, the great kingdoms of central Java had embraced Islam, although with somewhat less fervor than was true in northern coastal regions. By the time the first Europeans sailed to Java more than two centuries later, Islam was already well established. As European influence in trade and administration deepened in the first centuries of colonial rule, Islam increasingly became the rallying point and major counter–force for traditionalist, irredentist and proto–nationalist forces opposing the intrusion of foreign control of the area. Paradoxically, the fanatical commitment of intrusive European powers to engage Indonesian Islamic forces often led to the extension of this faith into areas of the archipelago that had been unaffected by the teaching of the Prophet Muhammad prior to 1511.

The extension of Netherlands East Indies control over the region was a long and fitful process that extended from the early sixteenth century to the first decade of the twentieth. In the early centuries of Dutch commercial intercourse with coastal trading states, competing British, Portuguese, Spanish, French and even Danish powers made an impact on selected regions of Indonesia. Dutch trading acumen, diplomatic skill and persistent interest ultimately allowed the Netherlands to prevail. The political and cultural coherence that gives form and substance to the term Indonesia hardly existed in the early years of Dutch influence in Java and Sumatra, however. Warring sultanates and fiefdoms were slowly brought under Dutch control, mostly by the device of indirect rule, in which honors, monies and superficial administrative privileges were bestowed upon native rulers in exchange for monopoly trading privileges. For over two hundred years, Dutch interests in Southeast Asia were represented not by the crown but by the Netherlands East Indies Trading Company. Representatives of this consortium of trading firms developed Batavia as a port and center of commercial activity, outfitted private navies and armies and slowly extended their influence across Java and Sumatra and into the far–flung outer–island regions. Only with the dawn of the nineteenth century was the influence and prestige of this trading company supplanted by that of the Netherlands East Indies Government.

The Dutch were content to rule through local regents. They assembled competent armies officered by Dutch professionals but staffed largely by minority outer islanders who had no intrinsic loyalty to the increasingly compromised courts of coastal and central Java. An export economy was established in which crops such as opium, sugar, indigo, coffee, cloves, mace, nutmeg, rubber and copra were nurtured, assembled and traded through monopoly control to advance the cause of the Company first and then the Dutch government. The village economy was fundamentally altered by the interests of the occupying Europeans. Javanese farmers, for example, were often forced to cultivate sugar, thereby reducing their ability to expand rice and food crops on their lands. Sumatran villagers were encouraged to work on rubber plantations; and, when they proved unequal to the task, laborers from more densely populated Java were imported to secure adequate production.

The extension of Dutch control over the East Indies was to some extent an unplanned process. Their intrusion as a technologically superior foreign power into local politics shifted the indigenous system of political alliances, radically altered patterns of intra–island and international trade and invested a new superordinate expatriate elite into the previously highly stratified social world of Java. The Dutch were content to leave the great majority of the native population in traditional village locales, and only select members of the noble elite group were educated in urban Dutch–language schools in preparation for subordinate roles in the colonial bureaucracy.

European colonial governments in tropical Asia ultimately foundered on the fundamental paradox of indirect rule. Because the number of Dutch colonial officials and expatriate residents in the Indies never amounted to more than a fraction of the indigenous population, considerable human resources had to be managed domestically to ensure the functioning of the colonial state, economy and society. By the dawn of the twentieth century, the first students from the Indies were on their way to Europe to undertake advanced training in the Netherlands. This handful of young Javanese and Sumatrans was exposed to the currents of contemporary western history at the same time that significant nationalist sentiments were coalescing among Muslim and secularist–nationalist groups sequestered deep within indigenous village society. Revolts and rebellions were constantly confronted and suppressed over the centuries of colonial rule, yet the spirit of independence and rebellion was never thoroughly quashed by the Dutch. Few such movements, which were largely nativistic insurrections against alien control, presented serious challenges to European authority.

In the twentieth century, the western–trained Indonesian intellectuals joined with village–based social, cultural and religious organizations to give birth to an unprecedented nationalist movement that ultimately succeeded in restoring indigenous control to the archipelago. Forging a nationalist movement in the face of active hostility from a colonial government is difficult in most circumstances. Indonesian nationalist leaders were faced with the task of creating a national entity out of a multitude of distinct cultures that had never in the past been truly unified under one political banner, had never shared a distinct common language and had rarely succeeded in bringing more than a few dispersed island kingdoms under unitary rule. Nevertheless, there were historical precedents and cultural norms that facilitated the process of national union. The great Javanese kingdom of

Onnes Kurkdjian

Laboratory of the Dutch Djatinroto II sugar factory,

East Java, 1924.

Madjapahit had brought states in Sumatra, Borneo and Sulawesi under its overlordship centuries before the Dutch appeared on the scene. Traders emanating from ports in eastern Sumatra and the Malay Peninsula had succeeded in implanting their language as a lingua franca throughout the Indonesian islands. The very fact of Dutch colonial control, which by 1906 extended from Aceh in northern Sumatra to western New Guinea, enhanced the patriotic consciousness of Indonesian nationalists. Working against the national movement was the ease with which the colonial government had been able to manipulate indigenous ethnic antagonisms to Dutch advantage.

Despite suppression by the Dutch, the nationalist movement grew in the early decades of the twentieth century. Marxist, Muslim and secular nationalist ideologies accommodated alternate views of the world. Javanese, Sumatran and a host of minor ethnic groups set aside ancient antagonisms and accepted the goal of forging an anti-colonial independence movement. A national language, based on Malay, was adopted in the 1920s. Modern nationalist organizations developed and intermittent revolts erupted, but it seemed that not even these advances could impact the mystique of European invincibility in the Indies. Within weeks of the outbreak of World War II, however, the myth of colonial destiny that the Dutch, British and French had carefully nurtured over the centuries in Southeast Asia was destroyed. Japan moved into the Netherlands East Indies shortly after Pearl Harbor; and, by mid–1942, all Dutch forces had been defeated and Dutch nationals were relocated in concentration camps manned by Japanese soldiers.

Occupying Japanese forces made good on pre–war promises to train Indonesians in military arts. By the end of the war, the Japanese had exported tens of thousands of forced laborers from Java to work sites across Southeast Asia. Few such *romusha* returned from the labor camps, although, with the exception of Irian (West New Guinea) and the northern Moluccas (Morotai Air Base), little actual fighting transpired on the ground in Indonesia. The Japanese land armies were virtually intact at the end of the war, and many Japanese soldiers turned their weapons over to Indonesian cadets. Indeed, Japanese military leaders encouraged Sukarno, the first president of Indonesia, to declare independence prior to the Japanese capitulation in Tokyo Bay.

The surrender of Japan ushered in a bitter period of prolonged warfare in several former colonial regions of Southeast Asia. In Indonesia, the Dutch attempted to reclaim their colony by force of arms, sailing on British warships from safe haven in Australia in the weeks just after the Japanese surrender. In November and December 1945, in the city of Surabaya, British and Dutch troops engaged in bitter armed clashes with Indonesian nationalists who were determined to defend their newly independent homeland. The Indonesian revolution lasted for nearly five years, ending in the last weeks of 1949 with the transfer of sovereignty from the Netherlands to the independent Republic of Indonesia.

The artistic heritage of Indonesia encompasses almost all traditional arts known to man. Depictions of daily life are found on woven leaf tapestries, in designs etched in wood and on textiles embellished by means of painting, batik or *ikat* dyeing or embroidery. Sculpture in clay, rice paste, wood and stone and casting in bronze and precious metals comprise yet further dimensions of the imaging of Indonesia in the context of traditional village culture. The many cultures of Indonesia, ranging from the high civilizations of the Hindu–Buddhist courts of Java and Sumatra in pre–colonial times to small bands of hunters and gatherers that still persist in the rapidly diminishing rainforest have long fashioned images of the environment, man, domestic animals and the supernatural with materials at hand.

Although photography entered Indonesia from afar and was borne necessarily on the wings of colonial enterprise, it has also contributed to the process of the imaging of Indonesia. The power of photographic images was immediately recognized by Indonesian rulers and petty princes who, early on, commissioned portraits of their families and courts. Photography also became an important medium for the validation of the colonial enterprise in the Netherlands as popularly oriented Dutch–language publications extolled the virtues of European administration while exploring the cultural and geographical diversity of the great tropical archipelago. *Toward Independence* concludes with photographs by Henri Cartier–Bresson taken as Indonesia emerged from colonial domination some forty years ago. Since that time, photography in Indonesia has, as elsewhere around the world, taken root as an essential element of daily life. Few major life crisis rites, be they weddings, circumcisions or funerals, transpire in Indonesia today without being recorded photographically by professionals or family members. Indeed, indigenous video specialists in Bali and in Tana Toraja have become a new and essential element in the planning, budgeting and documentation of major traditional rituals.

Images of Indonesia expressed in traditional arts such as incised wood, woven leaves, *ikat* textiles, painted panels and sculpted stone reflect indigenous perceptions of the universe. Early photographic images of Indonesia reflect Eurocentric visions of colonial society. The photographs presented here conclude at a point in modern Indonesian history when the legacy of the colonial past was receding and nationalistic perceptions of the present were coming to the foreground.

Adolph Schaefer

Ganesha, *Hindu Javanese stone sculpture,*
Batavia, 1845. Daguerreotype.

Adolph Schaefer and Borobudur

H. J. Moeshart

IN 1840, JUST A YEAR AFTER LOUIS JACQUES MANDE DAGUERRE HAD ANNOUNCED HIS REVOLUTIONARY PROCESS TO THE WORLD, THE DUTCH GOVERNMENT SENT JURRIAAN MUNNICH, AN ARMY OFFICER, TO THE EAST INDIES TO MAKE DAGUERREOTYPES OF BUILDINGS AND ANTIQUITIES. HE WAS LATER APPOINTED TO ASSIST THE ARCHAEOLOGIST W. A. VAN DEN HAM, WHO WAS DOING RESEARCH ON JAVA. THE REPORTS RECEIVED IN THE NETHERLANDS A FEW YEARS LATER about Munnich's photography were not good, however. The daguerreotype process is sensitive to moisture and temperature, and under the tropical circumstances very difficult to execute. Munnich apparently had too little knowledge of the process to allow for the difficult circumstances in the tropics. He complained that his landscapes did not succeed, probably because of the haze, and that he could not photograph small objects.[1]

Another daguerreotypist in the Netherlands, Adolph Schaefer, was a German who had set up shop in The Hague, where he advertised himself in the local newspapers in 1843.[2] His business did not flourish, though, and he offered his equipment for sale in early 1844. Schaefer applied to the Dutch government to be sent to the East Indies, and his request came just as news of Munnich's failure was beginning to reach the Netherlands. Ph. F. von Siebold, advisor to the Ministry of the Colonies, recommended that Schaefer's offer be accepted, thinking that the Dutch in the colony could have their pictures taken and that Schaefer might be successfully employed to document the antiquities of the island of Java. This arrangement provided the opportunity to send a professional photographer to the Indies, and the Minister of the Colonies welcomed this chance to replace the "amateur" Munnich.[3] The plan was that the government would pay for Schaefer's voyage and equipment and that he would be allowed to repay the borrowed funds by making daguerreotypes.

Schaefer received a large sum of money to go to Paris to buy new equipment and to visit Daguerre for some first–hand instruction. According to Schaefer, Daguerre took great interest in Schaefer's plan to photograph in the tropics and taught him some new techniques. Schaefer spent a total of more than 4,000 guilders on equipment, chemicals and plates,[4] and when he departed from the Netherlands, he had with him ten wooden crates and forty–nine tin cans with chemicals and silvered plates.

Schaefer arrived in Batavia, on the island of Java, in June 1844. For some time, nothing was heard from him, except for an interview in the *Javaasche Courant*,[5] according to which he had given a successful demonstration of his art. The government decided he should pay back the borrowed money promptly, and he was ordered to photograph the statues in the collections of the Bataviaasch Genootschap voor Kensten en Wetenschappen (Batavian Society of Arts and Sciences). The prices Schaefer asked for his photographs were, according to the government, much too high. He demanded 120 to 150 guilders per daguerreotype, while prices of 10 to 15 guilders were usual in Europe. It was decided to pay Schaefer a total of 800 guilders, and in April 1845 he was ordered to "start without delay" to photograph the archaeological objects of the Bataviaasch Genootschap.

Once this work was completed, Schaefer was directed to go to the Residence Surakarta, where he presented himself to W. A. van den Ham, the archaeologist. In September 1845 Schaefer departed from Batavia with his horses and cases for a ride of 450 kilometers to the Residence Kadu, where he started photographing Borobudur, the great Buddhist temple, under van den Ham's direction. To get there, he was allowed the free use of the post-office horses, a necessity because of the amount of luggage he had. Once at Borobodur, he started documenting the intricate bas-reliefs carved into the stone corridors of the structure. He was to get an extra salary for this work to pay for his expenses, but the amount would not be determined until after he had made six pictures and sent them to the government. His monthly salary was ultimately raised to 600 guilders.

At the end of 1845, the Resident of Kadu informed the Governor-General of the Dutch Indies that Schaefer had given him thirteen frames, in which fifty-eight daguerreotypes of Borobudur had been mounted. In a memorandum, Schaefer outlined the troubles he had making these daguerreotypes. The preparation of the plates, which Schaefer did himself, was made very difficult under his existing circumstances. There was no suitable space for a darkroom in the house that had been set aside for his use, and wind and dust could enter freely into the traditional, open building. Schaefer asked that a European house be built with doors and windows that could be closed, and in which an adequate darkroom could be made.

Making the pictures themselves was even more difficult because the narrow corridors in Borobudur made it impossible to get the appropriate distance between his camera and his subjects. The focal lengths of his lenses were too long to focus on the extended stone bas-reliefs in the narrow corridors, and he was not able to show a complete bas-relief in a single daguerreotype. Schaefer solved this problem by making several daguerreotypes and mounting them next to each other in a frame, but when he sent the daguerreotypes to van den Ham for his opinion, the archaeologist had much to criticize. For scientific purposes, he insisted that the bas-reliefs should be photographed in their original sequence. Van den Ham felt that the composite pictures did not give an effective impression of the real structures.

Schaefer estimated that to photograph all the reliefs on Borobudur, 4,000 to 5,000 plates would be necessary, and four to five years of work would be required. He was prepared to undertake this task, but only under certain conditions. He wanted to be employed as a civil servant by the government of the Indies, with either a pension for him and his family or payment of 150,000 guilders in monthly installments during the work.[6] This was an enormous sum for the period, beyond the financial capabilities of the colony. Also, it was difficult for the government to justify employing a photographer at that time since photography had not yet gained an accepted position as a part of daily life. Schaefer suggested publishing his daguerreotypes as engravings as a means of raising the money for the project, but this offer was not accepted. By this time, van den Ham had died; and, with scientific direction of Schaefer's work no longer possible, the Governor-General decided to stop the project. Schaefer was told to move to Samarang, establish himself there as a photographer and start paying back his debts to the government, an amount that had grown to 24,000 guilders.

With this move, the final part of Schaefer's unfortunate sojourn in Java began. In the succeeding years, it became clear that repaying his debt would be impossible. Samarang did not have enough European inhabitants to supply the number of customers necessary for a successful portrait business; and, in the summer of 1848, the Resident of Samarang informed the Governor–General that Schaefer had earned very little in previous months. He was considered to be someone without means. Schaefer was allowed to move for a year to Surabaya, Madura and Sumanap to try his luck there; but, in August 1849, still not able to repay his debts, he returned to Batavia. The government sold his equipment at auction, where it brought only 227.11 guilders.

Nothing is known of Schaefer's life after this. The Governor–General sent his daguerreotypes to the Netherlands, where they were added to the collection of the Royal Academy at Delft. They were later donated to the Ethnological Museum at Leiden, and were later moved to the collection of the Study and Documentation Centre for Photography of the Leiden University.

The ill–fated enterprise by the Ministry of the Colonies and Adolph Schaefer to make daguerreotypes documenting records of the Indies was much ahead of its time. Despite the failure of the earlier poorly equipped amateur, the Ministry had hoped Schaefer would be better qualified, but this was fulfilled only in part. Even with his superior knowledge and training, the tropical circumstances made execution very difficult. Nevertheless, the beautiful daguerreotypes Schaefer made in Java stand as testimony to the skill and quality of his art.

NOTES

1. National Archives, Ministry of the Colonies, 3 November 1843, Nr. 3.

2. E. Mensonides, *Een nieuwe kunst in Den Haag*, in *Die Haghe, Jaarboek* 1977.

3. National Archives, Ministry of the Colonies, Letter of 5 May 1843, Nr. 25.

4. National Archives, Ministry of the Colonies, Letter of 16 February 1844, Nr. 21/96.

5. Javaasche Courant, Nr. 16, 22 February 1845.

6. National Archives, Ministry of the Colonies, Letter of the Governor–General to the Minister of the Colonies, 2 October 1851, Nr. 48.

Adolph Schaefer

Borobudur, view of part of the first gallery before restoration,

1845. Daguerreotype.

Adolph Schaefer

Borobudur, Bas-reliefs from the west outer wall, first corridor, first gallery,
1845. Daguerreotypes.

Adolph Schaefer

Balinese Hanuman, *or white monkey general statue,*
1845. Daguerreotype.

Adolph Schaefer

Balinese Rangda *mask,*
1845. Daguerreotype.

Woodbury & Page

Roads and canals of Batavia,

c. 1865. Albumen print.

Woodbury and Page *Photographers of the Old Order*

John Bloom

WHEN PHOTOGRAPHERS WALTER BENTLEY WOODBURY AND JAMES PAGE ARRIVED IN BATAVIA, JAVA, BY WAY OF AUSTRALIA IN THE FALL OF 1856, THEY WERE FOLLOWING AN ALREADY WELL–ESTABLISHED TRADITION OF GENTLEMEN ADVENTURERS IN THE COLONIES. THE DUTCH EAST INDIES HAD BEEN PROVIDING RAW MATERIALS—PRIMARILY SPICES, COFFEE, TEA AND TOBACCO—FOR THE TRADE ROUTES OF THE EUROPEAN EMPIRES FOR SEVERAL CENTURIES; and, in the context of this commercial culture, photographs of the colonies were a much desired commodity in the homelands. These record, or topographic, pictures offered an often misleading glimpse of life in "primitive" or "uncivilized" cultures, but they satisfied in Europeans a desire for the exotic and unfamiliar, a wish to be one step closer to the bestial. The seeming distance and objectivity of the photographs fed the colonial illusion of dominance and security.

The British expeditionaries Woodbury and Page met while sailing from England to Australia. After some photographic success in Melbourne, but still seeking a photographic marketplace that would provide sufficient support, they continued on to Batavia, the main port of call for the Dutch colony. Arriving there, they may even have found it quaint to find canals and small–scale railroads in this foreign land, although neither commercial device was native to the archipelago. The British, of course, were old hands at colonizing, but the geophysical transformation of the tropical landscape accomplished by the time–tested Dutch technology of canal dredging must have been seen as a marketable photo–opportunity for the firm of Woodbury & Page. To British eyes, the image would have been a double take—the Indonesian landscape, the presence of canals and the landscape represented as view, itself a seventeenth–century Dutch invention.

As a photographic team in the Indonesian archipelago, Woodbury & Page flourished from 1856 to 1861. The firm produced images of architecture, portraits of local dignitaries and, of course, the ubiquitous view. In 1859, with the arrival of his brother, Henry James Woodbury, to help with the business, W. B. Woodbury returned to England to secure a regular supplier of photographic materials. He also contracted with the London publishing house of Negretti & Zambra to market their photographs in England. In 1860, they opened a new studio, Atelier Woodbury, in Chiribon, Java. In addition to the portrait services provided by the firm, Woodbury made photographic explorations into the less settled inland regions of the island. Woodbury & Page also marketed and sold photographic equipment and supplies. As a key supplier, they had contact with the best–known photographers traveling throughout Asia and the Pacific, and they frequently published other photographers' images under their corporate imprint. This was a relatively common practice in the nineteenth century; and, in the case of Woodbury & Page, it makes positive identification of their work after 1860 very difficult.

In 1861, James Page left the firm for further adventures. There is to date no record of his activities after his departure. The following year, Woodbury's younger brother, Albert, arrived in the Dutch East Indies to help with the business. Walter B. Woodbury, who had spent seven years in the Indies, returned to England with his wife in 1862. It was following his return that he accomplished the photographic work for which he is best known—photomechanical reproduction and a 1864 patent for the Woodburytype.

Albert Woodbury took over Atelier Woodbury in 1870, and the timing of this transfer coincided with the end of the Dutch government's so–called "culture system." While the switch from the "culture system" to the "ethical system" related primarily to agricultural policy, one can only conjecture that the Dutch government (as had other governments in Europe) wanted to generate a body of visual documentation to attract investment in and support for the change in policy. With renewed commercial interest in the archipelago came more image–makers and studios—and thus competitive markets. Some of the latest–known images with the W & P stamp were made of the Krakatoa volcano on June 21, 1886. Eruption of this volcano, felt throughout the islands, was one of the most violent ever recorded, and documentation of this news event was highly marketable. Records show that the firm remained in business until 1910.

From its early days, the Woodbury & Page aesthetic was to a large extent determined by the needs of the marketplace the firm served. Individuals in portraits were often shown vignetted, but were always removed from any surrounding context. Groups were also posed in makeshift outdoor studios, and the glass negatives were scraped to remove any stray contextual information. Finally, the views are neat and orderly—nothing to upset the empirical sensibility of command and control.

Woodbury & Page

Lombok nobility in traditional court costume,
c.1865. Albumen print.

Woodbury & Page

Sultan Paku Buwono IX of Surakarta,
Central Java, c. 1865. Albumen print.

Woodbury & Page

Ratu Paku Buwono, Royal spouse of Paku Buwono IX,
Central Java, c. 1865. Albumen print.

Woodbury & Page

Gamelan orchestra of the Regent of Bandung, outside of the palace,
c. 1870. Albumen print.

Woodbury & Page

Group of Bettawi, the original inhabitants of Batavia,

1860–1870. Albumen print.

Isidore Van Kinsbergen

Seated Buddha Amitabha statue, west side of Borobudur,

c.1863–1866. Albumen print.

Isidore Van Kinsbergen *Photographer of Javanese Antiquities*

Pauline Lunsingh Scheurleer

DURING THE NINETEENTH CENTURY, THERE WAS A GROWING AWARENESS AMONG EUROPEANS IN THE DUTCH INDIES OF THE IMPORTANCE OF JAVANESE ANTIQUITIES, WHICH CONSIST MAINLY OF TEMPLES MADE OF VOLCANIC STONE HOUSING STONE IMAGES OF HINDU AND BUDDHIST DIVINITIES, SACRED BATHING PLACES AND CAVES CUT OUT OF THE ROCK. THESE SHRINES ARE ADORNED WITH DECORATIVE MOTIFS AND OFTEN WITH NARRATIVE RELIEFS. Other items of interest are small figurines of deities cast in bronze or precious metal; ritual implements made of metal, such as water vessels, bells, lamps, incense burners, mirrors and golden jewelry; records engraved on copper plates or on stones; decorative parts of domestic buildings; terra–cotta objects for domestic use; and manuscripts on palm leaves. These relics date roughly from the fifth to the sixteenth centuries.

The Batavian Society of Arts and Sciences (Bataviaasch Genootschap voor Kunsten en Wetenschappen), which was founded in 1778, played a pivotal role in stimulating research of these antiquities. Often with financial support from the government of the Dutch East Indies, the Society dispatched representatives to make records of these remains and included descriptions and drawings in survey reports. With the development of photography in the middle of the nineteenth century, it was only natural that the Society should look to this new medium to further its interests. In Isidore Van Kinsbergen they found the photographer they were seeking.

Van Kinsbergen had arrived in Batavia in 1851 to take up a position as an ornamental painter and actor at the theater. He earned a living during the day by painting the scenery of the stage on which he appeared in the evenings.[1] As a photographer, he was self–taught. A few years after arriving in Java, he had come across a book on photography by chance and decided to master this new craft. Early in 1862, he was asked to be the official photographer for a diplomatic mission to Thailand that was headed by the Secretary–General of the Dutch East Indies, Alexander Loudon. Later that year, he accompanied the Governor–General, Sloet van de Beele, on a trip through Java and Bali. The photographs he took on these journeys, which were made with the collodion wet–plate process, were shown to the Directors of the Batavian Society as evidence of Van Kinsbergen's abilities. They met with great approval, and at the end of 1862 he was commissioned by the government, through the Batavian Society, to photograph Javanese antiquities under the direction of an antiquarian, the Reverend J.F.G. Brumund.[2] Brumund, who had started his archaeological trip in May 1862, died suddenly in March 1863, but it was decided that the photographer should proceed on his own.

Van Kinsbergen sent his photographs back to Batavia in batches as they were made. He would go to a site and stay for some weeks or months to photograph. He soon found himself confronted by a number of unforeseen problems, the greatest of which was that hardly any of the antiquities were in a fit state to be photographed. His report on the condition in which he found the temples on the Dieng Plateau and the measures he took to improve them is recorded in the minutes of the Batavian Society.[3] Much of the plateau was now a swamp, although the ancient Javanese had apparently constructed a good drainage system. After some trial and error, Van Kinsbergen was able to dig an outlet for the water with the help of coolies. In addition, not only were the temples overgrown with masses of vegetation, but the ground level had risen by up to one–fourth of the height of the temples. Sculptures were often covered with dirt or tar, which first had to be removed. Also, many of the antiquities were hard to reach—on mountains or in dense forests—and the weather did not always provide the kind of light that was required. It took him a total of seventy–two days to take sixty–two photographs on the Dieng Plateau.

Only two–thirds of the job had been completed when his contract expired in May 1866, but it was extended for another year.[4] When that year was up, many "final notices" were still needed before Van Kinsbergen could be persuaded to complete his commission. When he finally delivered the last photographs, the entire committee was extremely satisfied with the result. It was decided that prints of each negative would be made and assembled into portfolios called *Antiquities of Java.* These were sent to King William III of the Netherlands, to the custodian of Javanese antiquities of the Museum of Antiquities (Museum van Oudheden) in Leiden and to learned societies in London, Paris and Calcutta. Arrangements were also made so that copies of the photographs could also be ordered by anyone interested.[5]

In spite of the almost endless delays in completing this job, the Society soon gave Van Kinsbergen another commission, this time to take photographs of sculptures and reliefs of Borobudur, which had not been included in the previous project.[6] Van Kinsbergen set off in April 1873 and finished the job on June 1, 1874.[7] At Borobudur he found obstacles such as loose stones and a thick layer of earth on the floors of the galleries, settling floors and defective drainage. After some preliminary excavation, he was rewarded with the discovery of about two hundred reliefs. A problem here he had not encountered before was the narrowness of the galleries, a peculiarity of the structure that others had also confronted. He assembled a stand that could be pushed in front of each relief in such a way that the lens was at the correct distance from the object, but even so the preparation of one negative sometimes took ten days.[8]

Van Kinsbergen's photographs generally met with approval. The Directors of the Batavian Society had continuing faith in him despite his endless delays, and they always applauded his work. The pictures were made known to a wider public beginning in 1876 by P.J. Veth, professor of ethnology at the Leiden University, in a series of articles in the popular journal *Eigen Haard,* each of which reproduced one of Van Kinsbergen's photographs as the centerpiece. Today, specialists in the field not only frequently use his photographs for reference, but often do so with admiration. The photographer's greatest admirer, though, was the archaeologist G. P. Rouffaer, who never missed a chance to praise his work. In a 1901 review of a book of the arts of the Dutch East Indies by E. A. von Saher, who had included images of plaster casts, Rouffaer made a special point of lauding Van Kinsbergen's photographs to the skies.[9]

There was one diehard critic of Van Kinsbergen's photographs, however, Dr. C. Leemans, director of the Museum of Antiquities in Leiden. In 1858, the Dutch government asked Leemans to prepare a book on Borobudur using the architectural plans, sections and drawings of the sculptures and reliefs made by F. C. Wilsen between 1849 and 1857 (these had been commissioned by the government after the failure of the daguerreotype experiment), a paper written by Wilsen, and a 1857 article by the Reverend Brumund. With great perseverance and after surmounting many difficulties, Leemans succeeded in completing his task. In 1873, the book, consisting of four immense volumes of plates and two smaller volumes of text, was published by E.J. Brill in Leiden. In a letter to the Directors of the Batavian Society, Leemans commented on the portfolios of Van Kinsbergen's *Antiquities of Java,* which he had just received. He said that the work was not complete and that he would like to receive the missing photographs. In general, he found the photographs too full of contrast in the blacks and whites to provide a proper idea of the objects, and he felt that a measuring rod should have been added in each photograph. Finally, as a general objection to the medium of photography, he remarked that the objects were shown from just a single viewpoint in a false perspective, which made it necessary to add plans and sections for clarity. Then he came to his real point: Now that his own book had appeared, why was it necessary to commission Van Kinsbergen to document Borobudur photographically?[10]

In the meantime, a third party had involved himself in the discussion. The well–known Dutch critic, Conrad Busken Huet, who lived and worked in Java from 1868 to 1878, had little interest in things Javanese, but he now took Van Kinsbergen's side. In a short and sharp article in the March 1875 issue of the *Economist,* he reduced the dispute to a simple statement: Leeman's work is pedantry, Van Kinsbergen's is art.

The only just criticism of Van Kinsbergen's photographic series is that they do not provide a complete survey of Javanese antiquities. He included many so–called Polynesian images that are of no relevance to Javanese archaeology, but these are, however, charming pictures. He also completely omitted photographing several important temple sites. On the other hand, photographs of archaeological importance, such as a dated sculpture of Ganesha, show this deity so charming in his compactness that it has become one of Van Kinsbergen's most popular photographs. It is also a good example of his technical control; he often blackened the background of sculptures without disturbing their form in order to make them stand out.

Isidore Van Kinsbergen continued to live and work in Batavia until his death in 1905. He became famous for his photographs of antiquities, but he also did popular subjects such as Javanese portraits and landscapes.[11] In the circle of Europeans living in Batavia, however, he was more famous for other talents. No major festivity was conceivable without Van Kinsbergen's support. He decorated the rooms and was the driving force behind each party. Likewise, he was the moving spirit at the theater. He organized and produced plays, and in 1875 he invited a French opera group to come to Java.[12] These pleasures of Batavian social life likely contributed to his delays in completing his photographic commission, but he was still the best choice to do it. There was no one more suited for the job.

NOTES

1. *Batavian Nieuwsblad,* 30 August 1901, 2.

2. *Minutes of the Batavian Society,* The Hague, 1862, 5–6, 40–41, 57–58, 145–147.

3. Ibid., 1864, 262–269.

4. Ibid., 1866, 158, 184, 249.

5. Ibid., 1872, 16–18.

6. Ibid., 40.

7. Ibid., 1874, 71.

8. Ibid., 71–73.

9. Rouffaer, G.P., *Monumentale Kunst op Java "De Gids",* vol. 2, 1901, 225–252.

10. *Minutes of the Batavian Society,* 1873, 102–106.

11. S. Wachlin, in *Toekang Potret: 100 Years of Photography in the Dutch Indies 1839–1939,* Amsterdam & Rotterdam, 1989, 183.

12. Praamstra, Olf, "Een Indisch Toneelstuk", *Maatstaf,* April 1986, 130–156.

Isidore Van Kinsbergen

Punta Dewa temple (c. 750 AD), Dieng Plateau,
Central Java, 1864. Albumen print.

Isidore Van Kinsbergen

General view of Borobudur with Dutch flag,

c. 1873. Albumen print.

Isidore Van Kinsbergen

Ganesha *with a crown, from Candi Bara (1239 AD), a Javanese Hindu temple,*
near Blitar, East Java, 1863. Albumen print.

Isidore Van Kinsbergen

Gupolo, *guardian of Sewu temple (780–790 AD),*
near Prambanan, Central Java, c.1863–1868. Albumen print.

Kassian Céphas

Side view of Borobudur, with seated Buddha,

1872. Albumen print.

Kassian Céphas *A Pioneer of Indonesian Photography*

Jan Fontein

UNTIL RECENTLY, THE NAME OF KASSIAN CEPHAS, THE FIRST INDONESIAN PHOTOGRAPHER, WAS SCARCELY KNOWN OUTSIDE A SMALL CIRCLE OF ARCHAEOLOGISTS AND HISTORIANS INTERESTED IN JAVANESE CULTURE. DURING THE PAST TEN YEARS, HOWEVER, SEVERAL SCHOLARS HAVE FOCUSED THEIR ATTENTION ON THIS REMARKABLE PIONEER AND HAVE TRIED TO PIECE TOGETHER THE DETAILS OF HIS LIFE AND CAREER. BORN FEBRUARY 15, 1844, HE WAS NAMED KASSIAN (Kasihan or Kasyian), a name with a somewhat depreciatory connotation, although it is possible for it to mean *beloved* or *precious* rather that *pitiable*, the most common meaning of the word.

Although Céphas' first name may be somewhat unusual, his last name is even more so. The name itself, as well as the manner in which it was acquired, reflects the social and religious background of the colonial period in which he lived and the circles in which he moved. Little is known about his parents, but according to an oral tradition current among his descendants, he was the natural child of a Dutchman, possibly one who worked in the postal service in Yogyakarta, and a Javanese woman. Although his father neglected to recognize his offspring officially, it seems that Kassian was adopted and raised by his natural father's family. This family of staunch Dutch Protestants may well have taken credit for the fact that Kassian became the first Indonesian to be baptized in Central Java, an event that took place in Purworejo on December 27, 1860. By choosing a town outside the territories of the Sultan of Yogyakarta and Susuhunan of Solo, the missionary who baptized Kassian remained in compliance with the strict prohibition against all missionary activities in the so–called Principalities, or *Vorstenlanden*. Moreover, by choosing the biblical name of Céphas, which is the Aramaic equivalent of Peter, the missionary complied with yet another government policy of avoiding Dutch–sounding names for converted Indonesians or Eurasians. A single name suffices for all Javanese, and it was only much later, when Céphas petitioned the colonial authorities to be granted equal status to European residents, that he expressed a wish to use his original Javanese name, Kassian, as a first name and Céphas as his family name.

In the obituary that appeared in the Dutch colonial newspaper *De Locomotief* (November 18–19, 1912), it is stated that Céphas acquired his photographic skills "as a boy." In view of the minimal number of photographers active in Indonesia in whose studio he could possibly have been apprenticed, it seems likely that he began his career working in the studio of the well–known opera singer and famous photographer Isidore Van Kinsbergen

(1821–1905). He is the only photographer who is known to have lived in Yogyakarta during this period. He resided there from 1863 to 1875, a time during which one would not have called Céphas a boy—unless, of course, the word was used in the sense of a houseboy.

Little is known about Céphas' early years. In 1884, when his name was first mentioned, he had already established himself as a photographer and was already the court photographer to the Sultan's *keraton* in Yogyakarta. It is unclear whether he had received this appointment through the intervention of his friend, the court physician Isaac Groneman, but the close association of these two men unquestioningly had a decisive influence on Céphas' career as a photographer. In 1884, Céphas took sixteen "photograms" for a book written by Groneman on Javanese court rituals, dances and regalia. A few years later, another book by the same author described the religious festivals and the ceremonial pageants and parades held in the *keraton* on such occasions. Céphas again provided the photographic record that constituted the principal value of these publications. As a court photographer, Céphas needed the Sultan's permission for such extracurricular activities; it was always requested and invariably granted. The Sultan even graciously consented to halt a parade for a moment to give Céphas an opportunity to photograph the procession. The documentation that Céphas was able to provide of the ceremonies performed in the *keraton* is virtually unique and of immense importance to our knowledge of late nineteenth-century Javanese cultural history.

In 1885, a group of Dutch residents founded the Archaeological Society of Yogyakarta. In that same year, its first president, J. W. Ijzerman, discovered the hidden base of Borobudur, with its reliefs illustrating the *Karmavibhanga*. As the processional path that hid these reliefs from view was dismantled, section after section, Céphas was commissioned to photograph all 160 reliefs before they were covered again. This complete record has remained until today the sole source for the study of these reliefs. Seventy years later some of the original negatives could still be used to make prints, but since that time they appear to have been lost or destroyed by moisture and mildew.

The second president of the Archaeological Society of Yogyakarta was Dr. Isaac Groneman, and it was during his term of office that the Society embarked upon its best known, but least appreciated activity: the drastic "cleaning" of the ruins of Candi Loro Jonggrang at Prambanan. By removing the detached stones from the central courtyard of this temple complex and throwing them all on one large pile, the over eager amateur antiquarians created an additional burden for the next generation of archaeologists who faced the task of restoring these monuments to their original glory. Groneman's controversial involvement in this ill-advised venture had one lasting, positive result, his book *Tjandi Parambanan op Midden Java na de ontgraving* (Candi Prambanan in Central Java After the Excavation). Again Céphas provided the most significant part of the publication, its sixty-two photographs of the temples of Prambanan and the *Ramayana* reliefs of Candi Siva. This painstakingly accurate and comprehensive record was of considerable documentary value to the restorers of these temples and their reliefs.

Céphas' putative teacher, Van Kinsbergen, had an outgoing personality and an artistic temperament. The native photographer, on the other hand, was more of a quiet force behind the scenes, a self-effacing Javanese. Even when he actually made an appearance, it was in an inconspicuous, unobtrusive manner. In one of his photographs of the north side of Candi Siva, the man standing in the doorway of the cella is none other that Céphas, himself—fifty years before Alfred Hitchcock. In all probability, his son Sem, who was to succeed him as court photographer, opened the lens for this image. Céphas also appears in several of his photographs of Borobudur.

The last recorded involvement of Céphas in matters concerning Javanese antiquities dates from 1902, when he alerted the authorities to the recent theft of sculpture from the Candi Plaosan, noting that tracks made by the wheels of the thieves' cart were still visible. It is likely that the object stolen was the beautiful head that was to appear in the Ny Karlsberg Glyptotek in Copenhagen in 1907 and that, at the present time, can no longer be located in the Danish national collections, to which it was transferred seventy years ago.

When we compare Céphas' oeuvre with that of his teacher, Van Kinsbergen, we cannot help noticing a marked difference in approach. Van Kinsbergen was highly idiosyncratic in his selection of themes and subjects. He appreciated the beauty of ancient Javanese art, and he photographed what he liked with no apparent desire to convey to the viewer an overall impression of the monuments. But his magnificent photographs of the reliefs of Borobudur even inspired Paul Gauguin, in whose paintings and wood carvings the figures portrayed by Van Kinsbergen appear time and time again. The value of Kassian Céphas' work resides first and foremost in the faithful record it provides of monuments and antiquities, of court nobility and ceremonial life in the *keraton*. Céphas was a man of two worlds. As an official of the Sultan, he became familiar with the language, protocol and traditions of Javanese court life. As one who had achieved equal status with European residents, he moved in their circles as well, equally at home speaking either Javanese or Dutch. Conscientious and fully aware of the importance of permanent records to posterity, he recorded what he saw as meticulously and completely as would an archaeologist. In this respect, he was far ahead of his time.

Kassian Céphas

A young female abdi dalem *servant to the royal court*
of the Sultan of Yogyakarta posed in a studio,
1880. Hand–colored photograph.

Kassian Céphas

Bedoyo Prabu Dewa dance, Sultan Hamengkubuwono VII's palace,
Yogjakarta, c. 1880.

Kassian Céphas

Wayang Beber *from the village Gelaran near Wonosari,*
Central Java, 1902.

Bâraboedoer 1872   N° 70

Kassian Céphas

Overview of Borobudur from the northwest, before restoration,

1872.

Kassian Céphas

Man climbing the front entrance to Borobudur,

1872.

Kleingrothe's Images of Technology *The Reassuring View of the Indies*

Peter Kors

IN 1885, EUROPEAN PLANTATION OWNERS AND THE DUTCH COLONIAL GOVERNMENT BEGAN MAKING THE COSTLY, LONG–TERM INVESTMENTS NECESSARY TO SUSTAIN THE GROWING TOBACCO INDUSTRY OF THE DUTCH EAST INDIES. ROADS, RAILWAYS, HARBORS AND GOVERNMENT BUILDINGS WERE CONSTRUCTED; AND MEDAN, ON THE NORTHEAST COAST OF SUMATRA, EMERGED AS A MAJOR METROPOLIS. THE INFLUX OF WESTERN EUROPEANS EXPANDED the presence of modern Western culture and increased the demand for professional photographers. Their visual evidence of Western prowess against an exotic background justified colonialism to the resident colonists as well as to those in the motherland.

The German photographer Charles J. Kleingrothe opened his first studio in Medan in 1889. After two years, he was joined by H. Stafhell, and the two formed a partnership that was to last ten years. Kleingrothe and Stafhell owned and operated one of the most successful photography studios in the Medan area, a region that had become known among photographers for its commercial potential. Besides their commissioned work documenting tropical landscapes and the architecture of Medan, they also distinguished themselves as portrait artists. The Stafhell–Kleingrothe studio was modeled after its European counterparts. Lit by a large window facing north, which gave it an especially clear light, the studio used a painted curtain for a backdrop. The person being photographed was usually placed by a table, chair or some sort of fence, which served to unify subject and backdrop. The photographer chose the appropriate backdrop and props and posed his subject in such a manner as to create a harmonious whole. One studio portrait by Stafhell–Kleingrothe, taken in 1891, depicts a group of Freemasons belonging to the Deli Lodge. Arranged in a dignified grouping, the subjects wear identical dark suits, each man with a ribbon and medal around his neck. Also in the picture are the various symbols associated with Freemasonry—a pair of banners, a hammer, a compass, a sword and a sun. A neoclassical architectural facade with curtained arches is painted on the backdrop.

Stafhell–Kleingrothe also photographed many outdoor events, and one type of these, the "bon voyage party," stands out as being peculiar to colonial life in the Dutch East Indies. These events were for administrators who were leaving for Europe, either on temporary leave or for permanent retirement. Stafhell and Kleingrothe were on hand in 1891 to photograph a party given for the Secretary of the Deli Company, F. Gransberg. The photographs depicting this grand occasion show large groups of European partygoers in sampans and other small river craft sailing up the Bindjei River.

In 1901, Stafhell and Kleingrothe ended their partnership, and the following year Kleingrothe opened his own studio on Kesawan, a busy street in downtown Medan. A photograph of the street shows, among the many shop shingles, one reading "Photography Studio, C. J. Kleingrothe." His specialty became the photographic documentation of the cultivation and processing of tropical agricultural products. Apparently inspired by the English photographer W. L. H. Skeen, who as early as 1864 produced a series of photographs on tea and coffee production in Ceylon (now Sri Lanka), Kleingrothe began photographing the various phases of the tobacco, coffee, tea, rubber and palm oil industries. In these elaborate photo essays he shows in great detail the complete cycle of production, from planting to loading the finished product onto cargo ships.

In the beginning of the century, Kleingrothe was commissioned by several of the largest tobacco plantations—the Amsterdam–Deli Company, the Senembah Company and the Deli Company—to produce photographic albums that would serve as visual annual reports. These albums illustrate and illuminate all aspects of colonial tropical agribusiness: the newly constructed bridges and roads, the residences of the administrators and their staff, the barns in which the tobacco was dried and cured, the tobacco fields and processing plants, the hospital, and the coolie barracks. The workers themselves were primarily shown as figures placed against a background of tropical vegetation.

Another large commission led Kleingrothe to document the construction of the Deli rail line. This resulted in an album of photographs called *Deli Railway Company*. The photographs depict the laying of tracks along the swampy coastal areas, railway stations and railway bridges dramatically spanning ravines. A panoramic image of the terminal station at Belawan conveys the feeling of an important railway junction: a walkway above the tracks leads to the harbor, where freighters and steamships of the Royal Packet Company, which provided transportation between islands, lay anchored. Kleingrothe's photographs symbolized the expansion of industrial civilization through the superiority of European technology and assured the viewer that colonial dominion would prevail.

C. J. Kleingrothe

Chinese coolies employed as cheap labor,
Sumatra, n.d. Albumen print.

C. J. Kleingrothe

Amsterdam–Deli Company tobacco factory,
Sumatra, 1885. Albumen print.

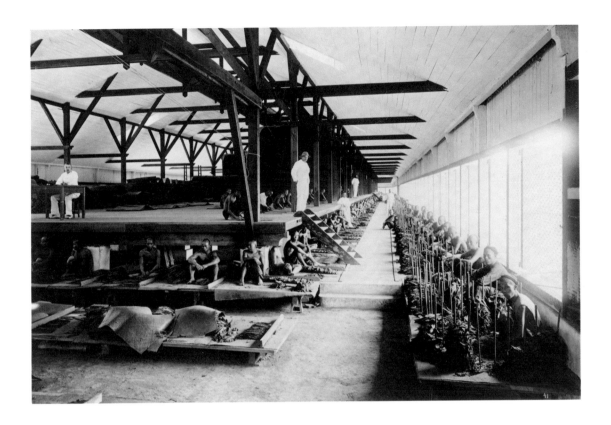

C. J. Kleingrothe

Amsterdam–Deli Company tobacco factory,
Sumatra, 1885. Albumen print.

Onnes Kurkdjian

Locomotive park of the Djatinroto II sugar factory,

East Java, c. 1924.

Onnes Kurkdjian *Viewmaker and Entrepreneur*

Hedi Hinzler

ONNES KURKDJIAN WAS BORN IN 1851 IN RUSSIA; HE DIED IN 1903 IN SURABAYA, JAVA. HE WAS A PROFESSIONAL PHOTOGRAPHER WHO WAS TRAINED IN TBILISI, MOSCOW AND VIENNA, AND LIKE MANY ARMENIANS OF THE TIME, HE WENT TO THE EAST IN SEARCH OF WORK. HE SETTLED IN SURABAYA, A PORT TOWN ON THE EAST END OF JAVA, IN 1884. FROM 1890 ONWARDS HIS NAME IS CONNECTED WITH A PHOTOGRAPHIC ATELIER THAT, IN ITS EARLY PERIOD, was located at the Bultzingslowenplein. While Kurkdjian primarily made portrait studies of Europeans in and around Surabaya and of Javanese women, he also photographed tropical forests, trees and volcanos. Kurkdjian's photographic style was characterized by the use of larger–format cameras to produce images of great clarity. In many senses, his work looks like that of the typical professional studio photographer working at the turn of the century. His portraits were printed on a textured matte surface, while views and record photographs were printed on glossy surfaces that were frequently ferrotyped. Kurkdjian received commissions, but produced work for promotional purposes as well. One such example is the *Queen's Album,* which was made to commemorate Queen Wilhelmina's visit to Java on August 31, 1898. This album includes views of the parade preparations, the visit itself and much of the pomp and circumstance that surrounded it. The images were mounted into an elaborate and decorative velvet–covered, silver–stamped album that Kurkdjian produced as a presentation piece for the Queen.

In 1897, Kurkdjian took on an English assistant, G. P. Lewis. When he was invited by the Dutch Government to photograph the eruption of the volcano Kelut on June 6, 1901 (the initial eruption took place on May 23 of that year), his assistant made the famous photograph of Kurkdjian at work, standing behind his tripod–mounted camera. Because it was so cold in the mountainous area, Kurkdjian was clad as for a European winter. After 1900, Kurkdjian cooperated closely with his associate; the Kurkdjian Atelier changed its name to Kurkdjian, O. & Co. Limited, and moved into new quarters in Surabaya. After Kurkdjian's death in 1903, G. P. Lewis remained in charge; and, in 1904, the Atelier became a "Company for the Exploitation of the Photographic Atelier Kurkdjian." In 1915, the Company was taken over by the pharmaceutical importers Mieling & Co. Portraits were the primary business of the studio after Kurkdjian's death, but views were also made. During the period from 1914 to 1917, while World War I was raging in Europe, Eastman Kodak Company, of Rochester, New York, became the primary supplier of photographic goods in the archipelago. While the number of professional photographic studios grew slowly, the use of photographic equipment by amateurs increased exponentially. Atelier Kurkdjian was Kodak's sole agent in East Java, and it thus provided developing, printing and enlarging services for many of the new users.

Onnes Kurkdjian

Ceremonies to welcome Queen Wilhelmina to Java,
August 31, 1898.

Onnes Kurkdjian

Street scene,

Batavia, n.d.

Onnes Kurkdjian

Plantation workers tapping liquid rubber,
Sumatra, n.d.

Onnes Kurkdjian

Volcanic crater of Bromo,

East Java, n.d.

C. B. Nieuwenhuis

People gathered at pasar *(market) at Bukittinggi (Fort de Kock),*
Sumatra, 1907.

C. B. Nieuwenhuis' Views of Sumatra

Anneke Groeneveld

C. B. NIEUWENHUIS WAS A DUTCH PHOTOGRAPHER ACTIVE IN SUMATRA FROM ABOUT 1890 UNTIL HIS DEATH ON APRIL 20, 1922.[1] ONCE ESTABLISHED THERE, HE QUICKLY CAME TO BE CONSIDERED ONE OF THE ISLAND'S BEST PHOTOGRAPHERS. HIS FAME DEPENDED LARGELY UPON HIS OUTSTANDING VIEWS OF THE SUMATRAN LANDSCAPE, BUT LANDSCAPE PHOTOGRAPHY IS ONLY ONE THEME IN HIS VARIED BODY OF WORK. A MAN OF GREAT TALENT, Nieuwenhuis kept up with technical developments of the medium and adapted his business to changes in the consumer market for photographs.

Christiaan Benjamin Nieuwenhuis was born in Amsterdam on July 4, 1863. He spent his youth in Amsterdam, and in 1883 he moved to Hardervijk. His early training in music enabled him to travel to Jakarta, following a young woman, Frederika J. S. van Ginkel, whom he had met during her leave in the Netherlands. He is reported to have left for Jakarta in 1884 as a member of the Royal Military Band. It was there, a few years later, that he learned photography at the studio of Koene & Co., which had been opened in mid–1887. It is not known how long Nieuwenhuis stayed in Jakarta, but it may have been until at least 1888.

By 1892, he had moved to Padang, Sumatra, where he set up his own studio in the side room of the house he designed and built at the Bentegweg. He married Frederika the following year. He placed a sign advertising his studio on the front of the house, exhibited his pictures on the outer veranda and ran advertisements in local newspapers. He made studio portraits in the carte–de–visite, cabinet and boudoir formats, using the more sensitive gelatin dry plates and faster lenses to shorten the posing time for his subjects. His customers were both Europeans and well–to–do native residents; he also received commissions to make official group portraits of Dutch colonial authorities.

In addition to making these portraits, Nieuwenhuis also sold views of Sumatran landscapes and towns that he made during photographic excursions into the countryside. He traveled extensively throughout Sumatra, from Sabang in the upper north to Palembang in the south. He consistently took his pictures from elevated and distant points in order to get overall views; street scenes of towns are rarely found. Nieuwenhuis' views show the contrasts of colonial influence and traditional life on the island. Some images that were especially popular among tourists depict only the forms and beauty of the landscape, but many illustrate his interest in showing the technical achievements of the modern time. He often photographed iron bridges and harbor yards, as well as the West Sumatran railway line and its stations.

The photographer also had an interest in ethnographic subjects he came across on his travels, and he made architectural views in Batak and Minangkabau villages. Locals posed for him with their tools and utensils, in their traditional dress, and Nieuwenhuis made some excellent anthropological group portraits. At one point prior to 1897, he received an assignment from the Dutch colonial government to photograph on the Mentawai Islands, on the west coast of Sumatra. On occasions such as this he took anthropological pictures for his own use. In an account of his trip, Nieuwenhuis says that he found it difficult to photograph there since the people had not yet had contact with photography and were distrustful of the camera. Nieuwenhuis distracted them with small gifts and had to work patiently, since they would not remain still for long. In one instance, he gave a *Radja* an old military uniform to convince the man to pose for him. Nieuwenhuis later traveled to Nias, where he portrayed nobles and warriors posing in their most precious attire and full fighting kit. Despite their general interest, the real ethnographic value of these pictures is clearly doubtful.

Nieuwenhuis also made individual anthropological portraits in his studio. These images show isolated native "types" of Sumatra and Nias in a European setting. He sold prints of these ethnographic and anthropological pictures, along with his topographical views, to Europeans as souvenirs of Indonesia. The sales extended his income from his commissioned work, and his photographs were soon published in popular travel articles and scientific essays.

Always looking for enterprising ways to extend his photographic business, Nieuwenhuis asked the military governor, Van Heutsz, for permission to join a military campaign in Aceh, where war had broken out between natives and the colonial army. During January 1901, he spent nearly two weeks with the Royal East Indies Army on an expedition to Samalanga. Nieuwenhuis and others had already taken pictures showing the military presence in Aceh, but they were static pictures of military settlements and portraits of soldiers that did not show the actual fighting. His Samalanga pictures are unusual because they were made while the conflict was going on. If his porters had not fled with his camera as soon as the actual man–to–man combat began, he would likely have taken pictures of the fighting itself, but he still can be considered the first actual war reporter in Aceh. Nieuwenhuis soon published an account of his experiences that included twenty–two pictures.[2] The images served then as propaganda for the Dutch Army, and today they are symbols of Dutch military superiority in Indonesia. In a 1902 review of the book, the images were praised for their informative value. Although the reviewer did not regard them as beautiful, he considered them an interesting alternative to the written reports of the war that enabled readers to get a real view of how things looked.[3] Later in 1902, Nieuwenhuis toured through Java with the amateur archaeologist Isaac Groneman to take archaeological pictures. Unlike earlier photographers, he depicted Borobudur and other temples in an artistic way, rather than presenting details for archaeological study.

By 1905, Nieuwenhuis had moved from Padang to Banda Aceh, and at the same time he advertised himself as a photographer in Medan. Medan was an important economic center where some of the best studios were established, including the Sumatran branch of Singapore's G.R. Lambert & Co. and the studio of Lambert's former employees, Kleingrothe & Stafhell. Nieuwenhuis did not want to miss economic opportunities in this center, and he traveled between the two towns. His studio was at the house of friends, the Reep family, and he stayed there several times a year. Nieuwenhuis' wife had died in 1898, and by this time he was taking care of his three children as well as his mother–in–law. He often took his children along to Medan to enjoy a holiday there and play with the Reep children. In Banda Aceh, his firm issued picture postcards with views and portraits of Sumatrans. After 1910, Nieuwenhuis moved back to Padang, where he issued a series of postcards called

Sumatra's Westkust (Sumatra's West Coast) as both photogravures and bromide prints. He also started reprinting and making enlargements of older views. This change in focus for his business was due to the growth of amateur photography, which lessened the interest in commissioned portraits, but the demand for quality views by professional photographers remained strong. In 1916, Nieuwenhuis photographed ethnographic artifacts from Aceh before they were sent to a museum in the Netherlands, and in 1918 he issued a portfolio, also called *Sumatra's Westkust,* that contained twenty–four photogravures of his most successful views.

In his later years in Padang, Nieuwenhuis made some excellent ethnographic and anthropological pictures of the Batak people. These differ from his earlier images in that they are more lively, showing people in action, at the market or dancing; they also show a more realistic vision of how life had changed within a decade. These images, in various sizes, were sold to tourists and were compiled into albums. Nieuwenhuis' daughters, Christine and Hermine, assisted in producing the albums. His elder daughter, Christine, continued to operate both the studio in Padang and the branch in Medan after Nieuwenhuis' death.

NOTES

1. Biographical information included in this essay has been taken from internal evidence in C. B. Nieuwenhuis' photographs, conversations by the author with Mr. and Mrs. Cornelis–Niewenhuis and with Steven Wachlin, and from the following sources:

    Maurik, J. van, *Herinneringen van een totok, Indische typen en schetsen,* Amsterdam 1897, 27–33.

    Anneke Groeneveld, *Toekang Potret: 100 Years of Photography in the Dutch Indies, 1839–1939,* Museum of Ethnology, Amsterdam/Rotterdam, 1989.

    Wachlin, Steven, *Commercial Photographers and Photographic Studios in the Netherlands East Indies 1850–1940: a survey,* Amsterdam, 1989.

    Zweers, Louis, *Sumatra, Kolonialen, koelies en krijgers,* Houten, 1988, 12, 105, 127, 160.

2. Nieuwenhuis, C., *De Expeditie naar Samalanga* (Januari 1901), dagverhaal van een fotograaf te velde, Amsterdam, 1901.

3. Review in *Tijdschrift van het Koninklijk,* Nederlandsch Aardrijkskundig Genootschap, 2nd S., XIX (1902), 436–437.

C. B. Nieuwenhuis

Group of villagers from the island of Siberut, of the Mentawai island group,

off the south coast of Central Sumatra,

c. 1910.

C. B. Nieuwenhuis

Nias warriors in festive dress in front of their adat *houses,*

c. 1900.

C. B. Nieuwenhuis

Bridge at Anai Kloof, Sumatra,

c. 1900.

C. B. Nieuwenhuis

Distant view of river in Padang,

Sumatra, c. 1900.

H. M. Neeb

Acehnese village chiefs paying their respects to Dutch colonial rulers,

c. 1905.

H.M. Neeb *A*
Witness
of
the Aceh
War

Anneke Groeneveld

THE ACEH WAR WAS THE LONGEST WAR OF THE DUTCH COLONIAL ERA. FOR CENTURIES, ACEH HAD REMAINED INDEPENDENT DESPITE DUTCH AND BRITISH ATTEMPTS AT COLONIAL EXPANSION IN THE STRAIT OF MALACCA, THE NARROW BODY OF WATER SEPARATING SUMATRA FROM THE MALAY PENINSULA TO THE NORTH. IN 1871, THE TREATY OF LONDON, AN AGREEMENT BY EUROPEANS NOT TO INTERFERE IN ACEH, WAS DISSOLVED, and from 1873 to 1914 the Islamic population fought against annexation by the Dutch, who initially occupied only the town of Banda Aceh. In 1904, a military campaign led by Lieutenant Colonel G. C. E. Van Daalen completed the occupation of Aceh.

H. M. Neeb, a military doctor, photographed the events of the campaign.[1] In his series of 167 pictures there is a clearly propagandistic theme that stresses the discipline and superiority of the Royal Dutch Indies Army (KNIL). Although perhaps unintended, Neeb's visual account also reveals the atrocities that resulted from the fighting. Within five months, almost 3,000 Aceh people were killed, more than 1,000 of them women and children. Roughly one–third of the region's population fell victim to the violent annexation which, only two years later, was condemned in the Dutch parliament.[2]

Hendricus Marinus Neeb was born in Muntok, on the island Bangka, situated off the eastern coast of Sumatra on November 22, 1870. His father, also a military doctor, was P. G. Neeb. Neeb went to the Netherlands to study medicine in Leiden; he joined the KNIL in 1892, shortly after he passed his exams. The next year he returned to Indonesia and started his medical career at the military hospital of Surabaya. He was transferred several times over the next few years.

In June 1903, Neeb was sent to Banda Aceh and was appointed to join the campaign of Van Daalen, which, from February 8 to July 23, 1904, took him through the regions of Gayo, Alas and Batak. Neeb was promoted during the campaign and was afterward made knight of the Militaire Willemsorde. Neeb stayed in Aceh until at least November 24, 1907, when he took pictures in Sidikalang. From then on he concentrated fully on his medical career; his only known late pictures date from 1910, when he attended an international medical congress in Manila and used his camera for his research on the organization of American military hospitals there. He practiced medicine and lectured until his death on September 15, 1933; he was buried in Bandung.

It is not known how Neeb learned photography. There is perhaps a link with C. J. Neeb, another military doctor who is supposed to have been his brother and who photographed during the campaign to Lombok of 1894. The earliest known H. M. Neeb pictures are from 1904, and they show that he was already a skilled photographer. J. C. J. Kempees, the aide–de–camp to Van Daalen, mentions in his 1904 book that Neeb's photographic equipment included a portable darkroom. He probably used dry collodion glass negatives that he developed, and perhaps printed, during the campaign.

It has been assumed that Van Daalen assigned Neeb to photograph the Aceh Wars, yet none of the contemporary reports confirm this, nor do they say that Neeb was especially trained to do so. The fact remains, however, that the pictures remained in Neeb's possession after the conflict. From Kempees' writings and from the detailed captions Neeb gave to the prints, it can be concluded that Neeb worked systematically, as if he fully intended to make a complete visual report. He included topographic pictures of the areas the troops marched through, showing natural obstacles like mountains and rivers. All bivouac sites were recorded, and fortified kampungs, or villages, to be attacked were photographed during reconnoitering patrols. It was technically impossible to take pictures of the actual attacks; but, as soon as a kampung was captured, Neeb went inside with his camera, following the sequence of the combat. He started by showing the points of attack and the fortifications and followed this with images of the indigenous victims overlooked by their conquerors. He photographed corpses from close range, with their wounds and distorted faces clearly visible. Sometimes even crying young children were still sitting or crawling amidst the victims.

It seems unlikely that Neeb's sole motive was to gather visual proof of the Dutch victories and superiority, although that is the inherent message of most of the pictures. The pictures recording the chiefs' surrender to Van Daalen would have served the same purpose, however. Propagandistic elements can be seen in his photographs of bivouacs, including those of his own field hospital, that show how well organized and disciplined the KNIL was. Neeb choose not to photograph demoralizing scenes, and military life was only shown from the heroic and cozy side. Wounded or killed KNIL soldiers were not depicted in the manner that the victims in the kampungs were; there is only a single picture of a military cemetery, one at Kuta Lintang with the troops' white dog sitting in the foreground as a symbol of loyalty. The conquered Gayo and Alas people are depicted either as corpses killed by the Dutch or as victims expressing their obedience to Van Daalen. Their faces, however, express obstinacy and distrust.

This balance of power is also reflected in pictures that Neeb took out of anthropological interest. He photographed the wedding of Si Pi Ih, son of a Kedjuron, a sovereign lord, who was loyal to Van Daalen. Neeb asked for permission to make a portrait of the married couple, but the bride and the women accompanying her, in accordance with Islamic tradition, were reluctant to pose. The women fled, but the groom forced the bride to stay, and even to unveil her face. The man might not have exposed his wife to such embarrassment if the other relationship involved were not that of ruler versus subject.

Within this context of Dutch domination and propaganda, questions arise of why Neeb portrayed the indigenous Aceh victims in the kampungs so realistically, revealing the shocking facts of the campaign; and why he gave priority to photography instead of first taking care of the wounded and the orphans, as might be expected from a doctor. As a military doctor, he may have been accustomed to wounds, death and violence. Impassive to the distress, he may have persistently continued his photographic series whenever his medical work allowed. If, in fact, Neeb was commissioned by Van Daalen to photograph, that assignment could well have superseded his medical duties and concerns.

Neeb's Aceh War images are an early example of photography's ability to encompass contrary meaning and intention. While Van Daalen obviously did not prevent Neeb from making revealing images, he may have also been indifferent to the losses, proud of his achievements and unable to comprehend the impact the images would have later on. Kempees wrote that the soldiers were amazed by the tenacity of the Aceh people, with both men and women fighting in festal attire, wearing ornaments and determined to fight to the death. Neeb must have been aware of the unmatched losses of the war. His general views showing the number of corpses in each captured *kampung* must have been intended to depict at what costs Dutch authority had been established. With these pictures, Neeb gave witness of the courage and strength of the people's will to withstand Dutch rule.

Neeb's photographs were soon presented to the public in the Netherlands and Indonesia. Kempees published twenty–eight images in his book, and the reviews were mostly sympathetic. In 1906 Van Daalen offered the Museum of Ethnology in Rotterdam 168 Neeb images. Today, these photographs still elicit feelings of shock at the events at Aceh, just as they did in the Netherlands nearly a century ago.

NOTES

1. Primary sources for biographical and historical information on H. M. Neeb and the Aceh Wars include the following:

Kempees, J.C.J., *De tocht van overste Van Daalen door de Gajo–, Alas–en Bataklanden,* Amsterdam 1904.

Stibbe, D.G. and C. Spat (ed.), *Encyclopaedie van Nederlandsch–Indie,* 's–Gravenhage, 1935, suppl. VII, 1407–1408.

Van Daalen, G.C.E., "Verslag van den tocht naar de Gajo–en Alaslanden in de maanden februari tot en met juli 1904 onder den luitenant–kolonel van den generalen staf G.C.E. van Daalen," in: *Indisch Militair Tijdschrift,* Sp. Iss.no. 14 (1909).

"Lijst van fotogrammen, vervaardigd door...H. M. Neeb," in *Notulen van het Bataviaasch Genootschap van Kunsten en Wetenschappen,* XXLII (1904) Bijlage XV.

2. Veer, P. van 't, *De Atjeh–oorlog,* Amsterdam, 1969, 267–272.

H. M. Neeb

Proud Dutch soldiers pose with weapons drawn during the Aceh War,

1904.

H. M. Neeb

Two Dutch soldiers standing by Acehnese storage huts,

while two babies cry among dead family members,

1904.

Thilly Weissenborn

Balinese women carrying water,

c. 1922. Photogravure.

Thilly Weissenborn *The Romance of the Indies*

Adrian Vickers

IF NINETEENTH AND EARLY TWENTIETH-CENTURY MALE PHOTOGRAPHERS ESTABLISHED A WAY OF SHOWING THE DUTCH EAST INDIES IN THE LIGHT OF A BENEVOLENT COLONIALISM BENT ON PRESERVING QUAINT CULTURES AND ESTABLISHING AN IMPERIAL SENSE OF SPACE, THILLY WEISSENBORN, THE FIRST MAJOR FEMALE PHOTOGRAPHER OF THE INDIES, INTRODUCED A FUNDAMENTAL TRANSFORMATION IN EUROPEAN WAYS OF SEEING THE REGION. Through her photography, she infused the earlier vision with a sense of the romance of the islands—the Indies as wish fulfillment. This warm, extroverted woman of dry humor and ready ability to make friends was more of a child of the Indies than she was Dutch.[1] She was born in 1889 in Kediri, East Java, of German-born, naturalized Dutch parents who owned a coffee plantation there, and later in Tanganyika. She spent less time in the early part of her life in the Netherlands than in Java.

The beginning of Weissenborn's photographic career is something of a mystery. One elder sister, Else, had studied photography in Paris and set up a studio in the Hague by the time Thilly was fourteen, and we know that the younger sister was working in the Kurkdjian studio in Surabaya in 1917. However, a number of Kurkdjian photographs later attributed to Weissenborn appear in H. H. Kol's momentous 1914 exposition of Bali, Sumatra and Java.[2] Most of the photographs in this book lack the warmth and glowing light of Weissenborn's later work in Bali; the poses of the men and women are particularly lacking the grace she brought to such images. For example, the image of two men beginning a cockfight is very stiff, the participants and surrounding gamblers are frozen, waiting for instructions from behind the camera lens. The man on the left, with a feather of a defeated cock under his hat for good luck, glances away from the supposed focus of masculine attention—the matching of cock against cock before one meets his death.

Weissenborn was trained by the Kurkdjian studio after the death of its Armenian founder. She worked under the supervision of the skilled English craftsman, G. P. Lewis,[3] and her apprenticeship included touching up photographs and a full range of technical work. The studio had thirty employees, European and native, and she was one of only two women.[4] In 1917, when she moved to Garut, in the nest of hill stations of West Java, she set up her own studio, "Lux." It was originally a part of a pharmacy owned by Denis G. Bulder, but she moved it to a separate location in 1920.

From that time onward, Weissenborn began to mark her work with a special lyrical quality. The views of her base at Garut all display the cool misty air of the quiet hills to which the overdressed and proper Dutch escaped from the sultry coast. The formality of the Governor-General's palace at nearby Bogor, the tenderness of

European mothers with their children and the uncertain spontaneity of colonial tennis parties provided her bread and butter at the time. More heart went into her long vistas of the hills and the scenes of mountain village life as a rural idyll. In these, she portrayed single native figures in the fore- or middle-ground of scenes that stretch out from comfortable Dutch gardens to distant volcanoes. In such views, she was seeking the magical qualities of the landscape, a special communion with nature that was different from what Europe had to offer.

In the early 1920s, Weissenborn brought the romantic qualities she had developed in Garut to bear on the mountains, temples, women and princes of the island of Bali. She became most famous for this work, which was produced for a new tourist industry the Dutch wished to establish. From this time onward, a range of magazines, books and pamphlets were put out by tourist authorities and travel writers. These were designed to attract travelers to the East Indies by showing the exotic cultures of the islands tamed by colonialism, which in turn saw itself as preserving lavish indigenous cultures from the depredations of the modern world. Although originally not considered important in the plans for tourism, Bali grew to be one of the keystones of that industry, and Weissenborn's photographs helped to give it that special aura by presenting its culture in the most exotic terms. In her Bali photographs, the tamed nature she captured in the hill stations of Java becomes one with the rich ornamentation of a temple gate, or blends into a sacred bathing place. A different kind of communion with nature, one centered around these lush temples and their art, made Balinese spirituality the epitome of the tropical East.

To combine nature and culture, Weissenborn frames her images of the baroque temple at Sangsit with frangipani branches, seeking similarities between the leaves of the ornamental silhouette and those of the tree. In a scene of an inner temple, she combines bright backlighting with the whiteness of ritual umbrellas and the holy gesture of prayer led by the Brahman high priest. The gestures of the assembled congregation move the observer's gaze upward to the sky as much as to the shrine, and they help to reinforce the clear break in the two halves of the composition. The seated humans emerge out of the shadows of the platforms and coverings at the extreme left, while on the other side the whiteness is reinforced by the plates on the middle shrines, the cloth around the shrine to which worship is directed and the offerings set on a raised platform in the foreground. The shapes of the plaited leaves of the offerings are similar to those of the palm and pandus leaves in the background, giving a strong sense of the naturalness of Balinese religion, despite its strange and culturally rich qualities.

The ideal spirituality presented in this photograph is also present in Weissenborn's romantic images of Balinese men and women. Unlike many of the male photographers of Bali in the 1920s and 1930s, she avoided the prurience given to images of Bali's bare-breasted women and was concerned with showing the women's dignity and self-possession. In her image of two women along a roadside, this dignity comes through in the erectness of the woman carrying the pot on her head, a stance emphasized by her thin, straight sarong and sash, the downward, half-embarrassed movement of the second woman and the line of the tree to one side.

Ironically, these same images were easily appropriated into the general idea of Bali as the *Island of Bare Breasts*, the title of a French novel of the time. Given the abundance of images of semi-naked Balinese women produced from the 1920s on, it is not surprising that Weissenborn was unable to change substantially the masculine bias of this generalized image, but she had a far greater impact with her best-known photograph, that of a young dancing girl seated before a gong. This photograph was frequently reproduced in 1920s Dutch tourist literature and has subsequently been in the literature that continues to flood out about Bali.[5] It captures that mysterious, ineffable quality of Bali—the inscrutable oriental culture of the island, rich but not threatening, that made it a place to which Europeans could escape from the drabness of their home.

Weissenborn's photograph of Gusti Bagus Jlantik, the intellectually able, short but handsome "self ruler" of the eastern Balinese state of Karangasem, captures her deep passion for understanding the inner spiritual qualities of the Indies through its exemplary characters. He was the Balinese ruler most favored by the Dutch, but also part of the new development of elite Indonesian self–assertion. One of a series of portraits of Javanese and Balinese aristocrats done by Weissenborn during the 1920s, the photograph captures his fully confident gaze directed back into her European camera, an assertion of a religiously and culturally confident leader of Indonesian society. His costume and setting display the nature of this indigenous leadership—traditionally Balinese in the widely–folded head–cloth set with a gold flower on one side and the flourish of brocaded breast–cloth at the front worn over a European–style jacket with Balinese ornamental gold edging. He is sitting on a gaudy European chair, a kind of extravagant statement in itself about the noble appropriation of European styles of display into an expression of local identity.

Extravagant princes, assertive and mysterious women and lavish temples combined with lush spreading landscape to make Weissenborn's Indies a place of dreaming romance. The romance was there to lure Europeans into a place so fantastic as to take them out of themselves. Bali served the narrow material interests of tourist development; but, for Weissenborn, her romantic photography was a way of telling others about the qualities of the Javanese and Balinese peoples and cultures that she had discovered for herself. She communicated the deeper spiritual values she read into the scenes and people she photographed.

NOTES

1. For further information on her life and work, see Ernst Drissen, *Vastgelegd voor later: Indische foto's (1917–1942) van Thilly Weissenborn*. Amsterdam: Sijthoff, 1983.

2. H. H. Kol, *Drei maal dwards door Sumatra en Java, met zwerftochten door Bali*, Rotterdam: Brusse, 1914; cf. Drissen, Vastgelegd, 10. 13.

3. Drissen, *Vastgelegd*, 12–13.

4. Ibid., undated photo, 13.

5. For images of Bali and tourism, see A. Vickers, *Bali: A Paradise Created*, Ringwood, Victoria: Penguin, 1989/Singapore: Periplus, 1990, see page 103 for an analysis of this photograph.

Thilly Weissenborn

Balinese cockfight,

c. 1920.

Thilly Weissenborn

Balinese praying in a family courtyard,
Bali, c. 1920.

Thilly Weissenborn

Gusti Bagus Jelantik, King of Karangasem,

Bali, c. 1923.

Thilly Weissenborn

Beiji *temple with ornately carved gateway,*
Sangsit, Northern Bali, c. 1920.

Tassilo Adam

Courtiers of the Sultanate of Paku Alam holding royal insignia,
Yogyakarta, 1924.

Tassilo Adam *The Photographer as Cultural Observer*

Kunang Helmi

IN AUGUST 1944, TASSILO ADAM DONATED A PORTION OF HIS INVALUABLE COLLECTION OF PHOTO-GRAPHS OF THE BATAK PEOPLE AND OTHER SUMATRAN ETHNIC GROUPS, TOGETHER WITH A COMPLETE DOCUMENTATION OF CENTRAL JAVANESE DANCE, TO THE ROYAL TROPICAL INSTITUTE IN AMSTERDAM. DESPITE THE FACT THAT ADAM HAD NO FORMAL TRAINING AS AN ETHNOLOGIST, HIS APPROACH TO PHOTOGRAPHY, AND LATER TO FILMMAKING, resembled that of an ethnologist, and the work he had done for the Dutch East Indies Government was valued as such. The collection spans fourteen years, from 1912 to 1926, and his Batak photographs, which had been registered at the museum in 1919, attest to his acute eye and thorough observations. It is clear from his photographs that Adam was infused with an appreciation and understanding of the Indonesian people he lived among for more than twenty–five years.

Born in Munich in 1878 to the German painter Emil Adam and an Italian mother, Tassilo Adam was destined to move to more distant and exotic shores during his seventy–seven year lifetime. Adam left Munich for further studies in Vienna at the tender age of sixteen. While still in Vienna in 1898, according to Adam's daughter–in–law, Elanore, he read a book about the Batak people of Sumatra. Fascinated by its contents, the adventuresome youth immediately decided to go there. The following year, at the age of twenty–one, Adam left Vienna to work on a Dutch tobacco plantation in Deli, near Medan, on the island of Sumatra.

Adam's stay in the Dutch East Indies was punctuated with severe bouts of malaria, among other serious tropical diseases. In "A Personal Experience with Malaria," published in the *Knickerbocker Weekly,* December 27, 1943, he recounted how he had resorted to a Sumatran herb mixture as a cure for dengue fever. In fact, it was out of concern for his health that Adam took sick leave and returned to Vienna in 1912; during this short trip he met and married Johanna. After returning to Sumatra with his bride, his health remained precarious, and he became adept at using traditional herb cures.

Tassilo Adam started to photograph when he came back to Sumatra, setting up a darkroom in his home in Pematangsiantar in 1914 and processing his prints himself. Due to the tropical temperatures, he had to resort to using buckets of ice to cool the water used when developing. Adam recorded much pictorial information about the ethnic group of the Kubus. He also spent some time researching the life of the inhabitants of Nias Island, off the coast of Sumatra. During his time in Sumatra, he collected many Batak artifacts, which he sent back to Dutch museums as a part of his ethnological work. Adam learned the Batak language; and, in 1948, he wrote the first book on Malay–Batak grammar with James Butler.

Once his studio was in place, what followed for Tassilo Adam was a very fertile period of photographic and ethnological research of Batak customs and physical surroundings, in particular those of the Karo Bataks. In addition to his photographic documentation, Adam recorded his impressions in writing; and, according to his observations, the Batak lived in constant fear for their *tendi*, or soul, the double of the ego, which was continually threatened by the *begus,* or evil spirits. Not only humans, but every living thing, including certain plants, had *tendis.* This was especially true of rice, their chief food. Basically a mystic who sympathized greatly with the Bataks, respected their culture and cared about the people, Adam did not have a typical "colonial" attitude. Perhaps it was this direct approach that contributed to the ease with which he gained the confidence of those he photographed. His portraits are of proud Batak personalities looking into the camera with admirable poise.

Adam became good friends with Pa Melga, the *sibajak,* or chief, of the large Karo Batak village of Kaban Djahe. One day he was invited to a great festival at Pa Melga's home at which evil spirits would be captured by a *sibasso,* a spirit–medium priestess. When she went into a trance, the photographer was ready: "My camera was set. A large amount of powder, which was necessary for a good picture, had been provided. But since it had become wet, I used a bamboo five meters long, attached to a cotton pad dipped in alcohol, to explode it. I shot six times so that the whole house trembled. It was a dangerous experiment; at each shot I fully expected to see flames."[1] One print shows the priestess, eyes closed and apparently in a deep trance, facing the photographer with the intense faces of seated villagers surrounding her.

One difficulty Adam faced was the Bataks' fear that by being photographed their *tendis* could be endangered. In one case, much to Adam's surprise and horror, a chieftain died three days after having refused to let Adam take his portrait, at which time Adam had said jokingly that he would get him dead or alive. Another time, a portrait he made of only the head of a chieftain of a headhunter tribe almost led to his own death. It was only when he returned with a full–length portrait that the chieftain was certain of getting his body back, and consequently the photographer was out of danger!

The Adam children, Lilo, Claus and Inge, were born in Sumatra and, despite many hardships, spent their early formative years growing up in an extraordinary and unpredictable atmosphere. In 1921, however, twenty–two years after Adam's arrival in the Dutch East Indies, Adam, his wife and their children, left Sumatra for Yogyakarta, Java, arriving there shortly after the coronation of the new Sultan. The Adam family was first the guest of the Dutch Resident, Mr. Jonqui'ere: "He, indeed, was my greatest teacher of Javanese habits and customs, of Javanese arts and crafts. He gave me every opportunity to witness and photograph religious processions, wedding festivals in the palaces, ceremonies on the anniversary of the Sultan's coronation, the beautiful *Serimpi* and *Bedoyo* dances, and last, but not least, the great *Wayang Wong* performances on both the Queen's Jubilees, in 1923 and 1926."[2]

Adam established a photographic studio in Yogyakarta, and he not only did commissioned portraits but, with the express permission and benediction of Sultan Hamengku Buwono VIII, he filmed and photographed court dances and rituals. He was not permitted to use artificial light for this work, however. Radically different from the harsh conditions in Sumatra, the highly refined civilization of Javanese Court life became just as familiar to this consummate recorder of the natives of the Dutch East Indies. Adam faithfully recorded, photographed and filmed the *Wayang Wong* theatre, the *Wayang Topeng,* the *Kuda Kepang* (Horse Dance), the *Serimpi* and *Bedoyo* Dances and Javanese Shadow puppets. Many of these performances were never to be repeated again to the present day. His precise verbal description of Javanese theater performances contributed greatly to the small amount of information available about this entirely different form of performing arts: "There is no stage, no settings, no curtain, no announcement of changes during the play, not even—as in Shakespeare's time—a board describing the scenery."[3] Capturing the beauty and dignity of these dancers, many of whom were of noble birth, Adam wonderfully portrayed them in their dance finery. Most of the costumes of the Javanese nobles, their everyday wear as well as their dance attire, were made of special hand–drawn batik. Adam's photographs are thus invaluable documents, since contemporary costumes are no match for their perfection.

As he had in Sumatra, Adam immersed himself entirely in Javanese life and beliefs, and he witnessed many more intimate aspects of court life in Central Java than had ever been revealed to westerners before. A prime example of this is the extraordinary photograph documenting the circumcision of a royal prince of the Susunahan of Solo, in which a white–gloved Dutch doctor protects the royal eyes while an attendant peers quizzically into the camera. It is unusual that both a doctor and a photographer would have been allowed to participate in an important ritual of the inner circle of the court.

In 1926, Adam contracted amoebic dysentery for the third time. For the sake of his own health and that of his children, the Adam family, sacrificing their deeply felt bonds to the East Indies, decided to return to Europe. He lectured in Europe, sold films and supplied pictures to German magazines. They spent some time in Salzburg, Vienna and Holland before moving to New York, where, from 1929 to 1933, Adam was curator of Oriental art at the Brooklyn Museum. The last years of Tassilo Adam's life—he died in 1955—were spent writing for American publications and attempting to return to Indonesia. Sadly, the Javanese of Yogyakarta had lost interest in him because they regarded him as an *Orang Belanda,* a Dutchman. Despite his obvious love for Indonesia and its people, Tassilo Adam died far from its once welcoming shores. His collection of photographs, however, remains a tangible reminder of his presence there.

NOTES

1. Tassilo Adam, "Batak Days and Ways", *Asia,* February 1930, 123.

2. Tassilo Adam, "Wayang Wong: the Javanese Theatre", *Knickerbocker Weekly,* September 1943, 25–26.

3. Ibid.

Tassilo Adam

A Sumatran Batak Sibasso *priestess in a trance ceremony,*

1919.

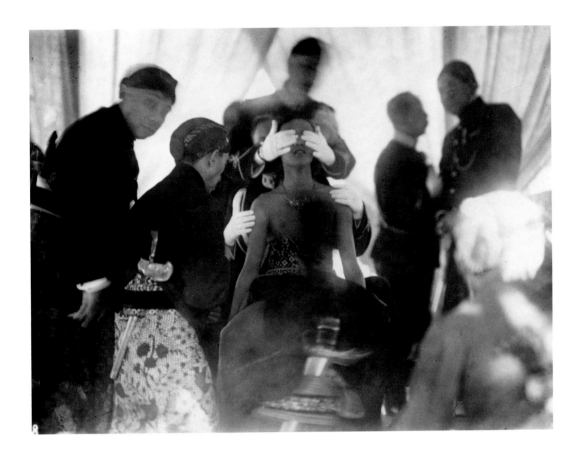

Tassilo Adam

Muslim circumcision ceremony for a royal Prince,
Solo, Java, 1925.

Tassilo Adam

Raden Wedanan Indramardowo
playing the Wayang Wong *role of Bambang Semitra,*

1923.

Tassilo Adam

Puteri Bibi Radjah, favorite dancer of the Sultan of Yogyakarta,

1922.

Tassilo Adam

Four Javanese Wayang Wong *theater clowns*
from the play Bagawan Mayangkara,
c. 1923–1926.

Tassilo Adam

Seven–year–old daughter of Pangeran Adipati Arya Pakoe Alam VII
performing the Srimpi *dance,*
Yogyakarta, 1925.

Walter Spies

A young Balinese Legong *dancer from Bedulu,*

1936.

Walter Spies *The Artist as Photographer*

John Stowell

WALTER SPIES CAME TO INDONESIA IN 1923 IN SEARCH OF A MORE GENUINE AND SATISFYING EXISTENCE THAN THAT HE HAD PREVIOUSLY EXPERIENCED IN GERMANY IN THE FIVE YEARS FOLLOWING WORLD WAR I. BORN IN MOSCOW IN 1895 INTO A WELL–TO–DO GERMAN FAMILY WITH WIDE–RANGING BUSINESS INTERESTS, HE GREW UP FLUENT IN BOTH GERMAN AND RUSSIAN AND WAS TRAINED TO REGARD THE GERMAN TRADITION AS ONE OF INTELLECTUAL, ANALYTIC THOUGHT, while his experience of Russia was of the worlds of nature and art. From 1905, winter meant academic schooling in Dresden; summer meant long holidays on a family estate at Nekljudovo in the Russian countryside. At the time, photography meant formal studio portraits of the family, but also snapshots of tennis parties and pet animals. With the coming of the war, the family was scattered and its Russian fortune confiscated. Spies spent three years in rustic internment at Sterlitamak in the southern Urals, living and studying the life of the semi–nomadic Bashkir, Kirgiz and Tartar tribes of the region. During the post–revolutionary turmoil, he made his way back to civilization. For some months he enjoyed the euphoric, experimental liberation of the artistic life of Moscow, when painters like Marc Chagall and Wassily Kandinsky came back to Russia to celebrate the dawn of a new age. But when life became dangerous for foreigners, he had to return to Germany and the penurious existence of the bohemian artist in Dresden and Berlin whose one rule in life was never to commit oneself to a system.

While he never received any formal painting instruction, Spies picked up many features of his later painting style from his friends Otto Dix and Oskar Kokoschka. At the time of their closest contact, Dix was making an intense study of the techniques of applying glazes characteristic of the Old Masters and using this knowledge in his own work. Spies adopted this method as his favored medium. The contact with Kokoschka was more personal than professional. Many people who knew Spies have spoken of the charm and grace of his personality; perhaps it was not just typical hyperbole when Kokoschka wrote of him that "when he left the room it was as if the sun went down." [1]

As a member of the Berlin avant–garde in painting and music circles in 1920, it was inevitable that Spies should come into contact with the world of film. A close friendship developed with Friedrich Murnau, and Spies acted as artistic adviser for a number of Murnau's major silent films, the best known being *Nosferatu*, the vampire film. It was no doubt his close observation and discussion of Murnau's filming techniques that taught Spies how to use dramatic lighting effects and unusual perspectives, stylistic devices he continued to use in his paintings and in the films he later helped others to make in Indonesia. Two dominant features of his painting style that may be traced to this early work on the film under Murnau are the compositional device of strongly emphasized diagonals and the concentration on tonal contrast rather than vivid color.

The failure of German society to achieve a new, viable and stable form in the post–war years, and its retreat into conservatism led many intellectuals and artists to emigrate, either physically or spiritually. Spies found himself stifled in the tense atmosphere of Berlin and talked more and more frequently of leaving. As a result of having made good friends in Holland with colonial connections, he laid careful plans to test life in what was then the Dutch East Indies. The initial impetus behind his decision perhaps stemmed from his discovery in Berlin of Gregor Krause's book of photographs celebrating Bali and its people.

After working his passage to Java as an ordinary seaman on a collier, it was not long before Spies found a position as director of the Western orchestra of the Sultan of Yogyakarta, a job that gave time for painting and access to the study of the Court Arts, including the instruments and music of the Javanese gamelan. Surviving prints in family albums from this time show that Spies used photography as an aide–memoire for landscape paintings, and his photographs reflected the rhythmic repetition of forms such as the lattice of a bamboo suspension bridge, or fixed the framed space of a body of water seen through surrounding foliage.

In 1927 he exchanged the delicacy and refinement of the Central Javanese court for the robustness and vigour of Bali. After several visits there, he moved to the upland village of Ubud at the invitation of the local ruler, Cokorda Gede Rake Sukawati. For twelve years, Spies seldom left Bali, steeping himself in the arts, customs and history of its people and becoming familiar with every facet of its physical nature. The discoveries he made found expression in paintings and drawings, films and gramaphone records, articles in learned journals and guide books. The greater part of his photographic records and written manuscript studies was lost when he was interned, again as a German national, during World War II. Eighteen months later, in January 1942, he met his death by drowning when the S. S. Van Imhoff, taking internees to British India, was sunk by a Japanese bomber off the coast of the island of Nias. In spite of the efforts by friends to preserve them, most of his papers and possessions disappeared during the Japanese occupation of Indonesia.

Nevertheless, the Dutch scholarly journals of the twenties and thirties bear more than a few of Spies' photographs of archeological and ethnographic subjects. His first camera was a Rolleiflex, which came to grief by tumbling down a gorge in Sumatra when Spies was scrambling over rocks in pursuit of a butterfly. This was soon replaced in late 1935 by the newest Leica, received from Victor Baron von Plessen as a partial payment for his work on the film *Insel der Demonen* (Black Magic), which had been shot, largely under Spies' direction, in 1931. Most photographs presented here were made during 1936 as illustrations for the book *Dance and Drama in Bali*, which he wrote in collaboration with Beryl de Zoete, a British expert on dance. Over one hundred photographs by Spies were included in that publication, and most of the original prints, along with others that were not used, were preserved when Beryl de Zoete took them to London. They eventually found their way to the Leiden University. As photographs of the dance, they fall naturally into several groups, according to the kinds of dance portrayed; but these groups also rather neatly illustrate the subjects, themes or concerns that moved Spies, both as a visual artist and as a musician. It is in dancing above all that patterns of space and time come together. We can here discern the straight descriptive element of the portrait; whether of Mario of Tabanan, creator of the *Kebyar,* in a pose from this seated flirtation dance, which apparently defies gravity in its folds and angles; or of the classical *Legong* dancer from Bedulu, where curve echoes curve; or again of the simultaneous relaxation and tension of the hobby–horse dancer in trance.

Another group involves dancers in formation, such as in the *Baris* (warrior) dances or in the *Rejang* temple dances. Repetitive patterning held a great fascination for Spies throughout his life, whether in music or the visual arts. For example, he found it perfectly natural that there was an underlying unity connecting the music of

Johann Sebastian Bach, the gamelan, the wing of a dragonfly and growth patterns of foliage, and he constantly returned to the question of how delight in the discovery of pattern in one sphere could find its echo in another. He drew and photographed the rhythmic ornament of Balinese palm–leaf banners *(lamak)* and the ebulliently florid carvings in wood and stone. When Balinese painters in the early thirties started producing a new style of work, there was a marked emphasis in work by painters from around Ubud, who were Spies' friends, on the rhythmic treatment of natural forms.

The third group of photographs depicts figures in a landscape, often dramatically back–lit, such as the *Rangdas* from the *Barong* play. The feeling for the theatrical that pervades Spies' view of Bali is displayed in the photograph taken in early morning light of the village of Trunyan on the shores of Lake Batur, where he had come to record a fertility ceremony. Light slants through the trees and across both the roofs of the hall and the throne for the gods on its pedestal on the righthand side. The roofs of these structures are in shadow and cast their own deep shadows, so that the brightly lit area behind is like a stage or screen awaiting some drama soon to be enacted.

We can readily observe that the early impulse from the films of Friedrich Murnau found one echo in the tonal contrast between deep jungle shadow and bright tropical sunlight of the Balinese landscape and another in the "moving pictures" of the *wayang kulit,* the Indonesian shadow puppet play; all of them contribute to the specific quality of the painter's style. There is an irony in the fact that Spies' surviving paintings are scattered around the world, most of them in private collections and thus not readily accessible. His public reputation as an artist rests to a great extent on the photographs in *Dance and Drama,* which were so carefully printed to his specifications.

During the thirties, photography was rapidly developing as a tool for the anthropologist, and it was Gregory Bateson and Margaret Mead who took photographic recording of the subjects of their field work to its limits. During their period in Bali from 1936 to 1938, they sometimes photographed the same performances and ceremonies that Spies had arranged to record for his book. When *Dance and Drama* was finished, Spies passed his camera to the anthropologists' colleague, Jane Belo, who was recording children and trance–dancers. Her husband, Colin McPhee, a musicologist and composer, was also a fine photographer with a great sense for rendering volumes. This group of artist–scholar–scientists compiled an impressive photographic account of Bali between the Wars, but for Spies, every record required transformation through the operation of aesthetic vision. He was above all a picture maker.

This is the way he was remembered by a friend from the Dutch colonial administration: *…the picture that springs to mind is that of the photographer I so often saw in the mornings on our trips to the highlands. As we sat outside our tent, usually placed to take advantage of a good view…he would suddenly seize his Rolleiflex and go off without saying a word to photograph the mists gleaming in the first light or smoke rising from the houses in the valley. I can still see his face before me as he watched with attention keyed to catch the awakening daily round of the village or the gentle sway of a cluster of giant bamboo stems overhanging a gorge. Incidentally this was an expression he habitually adopted when pacing around a subject he was about to photograph, muttering away to himself in concentration.*[2]

NOTES

1. From a memoir by Kokoschka in Hans Rhodius, *Schonheit und Reichtum des lebens, Walter Spies, Maler und Musiker auf Bali, 1895–1942,* Boucher, Den Haag, 1964, 119.

2. Ibid., Memoir by C. J. Grader, 357.

Walter Spies

Altar and pavilion in Trunyan village, on the shore of Lake Batur,

Bali, 1932.

Walter Spies

Rangdas *from the* Barong *play at Pagoetan,*

Bali, 1937.

Walter Spies

Kechak *dancers in a village purification ceremony,*
Bali, 1936.

Walter Spies

Balinese women at Tenganan dancing the Rejang,

1936.

Walter Spies

Mario, the legendary Balinese dancer, performing the Kebyar,
1936.

Walter Spies

Barong Landung, *a protective spirit periodically brought out of the temple,*

Bali, 1936.

Henri Cartier-Bresson

Batubulan villagers entranced during a Barong *performance,*
Bali, 1949.

Henri Cartier–Bresson *Primacy of the Other Over Fact*

John Bloom

PHOTOGRAPHY HAS CONVENTIONALLY BEEN PORTRAYED AS A RECORDER OF FACTS. IT HAS ALSO BEEN TREATED AS A SERVANT OF APPEARANCE, ITS IMAGES PLACED IN THE CATEGORY OF SCIENTIFIC KNOWLEDGE. BUT PHOTOGRAPHY IS SOMETHING OTHER THAN A RECORDER OF FACTS. THE FACT THAT PHOTOGRAPHER AND CAMERA SELECT SEGMENTS OF A CONTINUOUS WORLD SUGGESTS THAT THE IMAGE MAY BE JUST AS MUCH ABOUT ABSENCE—THAT NOT SEEN IN THE IMAGE—as it is about what is presented. The camera's instant, fully formed image is a facsimile that induces the viewer to forget real time and space and accept, instead, its illusion. Just as the world of spirits is as alive in the culture of Indonesia as the physical landscape, so too is the metaphysical reality that lies behind or adjacent to appearance in the photographic images made there throughout the past 150 years.

The credibility and power of Henri Cartier–Bresson's images are based upon his capacity to hold the rules of reality in suspense and to convince us of their irrelevance in the face of artistic truth. This capacity allows him to photograph ecstatic trance dances in almost the same breath that he reports on the political realities of a burgeoning independent nation. For him, these are extremes of human ritual which, because of their inherent experiential realms, demand different visual representations. The camera is simply the instrument that responds to his sense of the meaning of what occurs before him. Based upon the consistent intensity of his images, meaning is something other than the fact of appearance.

Henri Cartier–Bresson was born in Chanteloupe, France, in 1908. He became seriously involved in photography in 1930, while recuperating from an illness. He had been exposed to Cubist painting and to the work of the Surrealists prior to his photographic career; both art movements, as well as early cinema, were to have a profound effect upon his vision. He was also influenced by the photographers Eugene Atget, Man Ray and André Kertész. In 1932, Cartier–Bresson had his first exhibition of photographs at the Julien Levy Gallery in New York City and published his first photo–reportage in the French magazine *Vu*. The following year, he began using a 35mm Leica, and with its immediate response to his intuitive vision, he brought a new impulse to photojournalism. *Images a la Sauvette* (The Decisive Moment), the title of his most influential book, published in 1952, became the term given to his style, which is characterized by dynamic composition and a profound understanding of human psychology.

In 1935, he studied cinematography in New York City with Paul Strand; he returned to France in 1936 to work with filmmaker Jean Renoir. In 1937, during the Spanish Civil War, he made a documentary film, *Victoire de la Vie,* on the conditions in Spanish hospitals. Drafted at the outbreak of World War II, he was captured by the Germans in 1940. During his imprisonment, his Indonesian wife, Ratna, sent him a Malaysian dictionary and they were thus able to communicate secretly in her native tongue. Cartier–Bresson escaped from prison in 1943; and, later that year, he organized photographic units for the French Resistance to document the German Occupation. In 1947, with Robert Capa, George Rodger and David Seymour, Cartier–Bresson founded Magnum Photos, a cooperative picture agency. Throughout the remainder of his long and prolific career, he has traveled internationally to document important political and cultural events. Much of this work is characterized by a revelatory understanding of the relationship between people and their environment.

Indonesia held a special attraction for Cartier–Bresson since his wife is from Java. This personal link added depth, cogency and cultural sensitivity to an already existing alignment he held with the emerging independence movement headed by Sukarno. He had photographed in India both during its struggles to transcend a colonial past and at the sanctioning of its statehood after World War II. He recognized a similar political situation in Indonesia in 1949 and 1950. As his photographs of political speeches, rallies, departing Dutch soldiers and returning guerrillas show, he had a profound sympathy for the newly forming democratic state.

With the sheer beauty of the Indonesian agricultural landscape as a backdrop, Cartier–Bresson has photographed two quite separate realities in his portrayals of Sukarno's political campaigning and Balinese trance dances. On one level, they are complementary in the sense that the rhythms and changes of politics are a kind of superstructure that has little effect upon popular cultural and spiritual practices. Without text and an historical perspective of politics in a colonial country, the apparent self–inflicted violence of the trance dance— the expressionistic faces and intense gestures—makes the images of political change seem pale. Yet the faces and gestures mask a rather different reality. What appears to the onlooker as contortion and exhaustion is a ritualistic inner journey toward transcendence. Cartier–Bresson's images suggest this other reality through graphic configuration and the portrayal of support in those helping the dancers.

In the political photographs, Sukarno is seen happily campaigning from his shiny black car and speaking from a makeshift podium. The outward signs indicate an adopted political methodology and negate the kind of communal reality that lives within the popular culture. The servants are happy removing the Dutch artifacts from the palace, and the Dutch soldiers seem more than happy to be leaving. If there is a tension in these pictures of independence, it is that so much of what remains evident is Eurocentric in origin—including the new political order.

Cartier–Bresson himself noted his observations about the conflicting bases of the "new" politics and the existing social order in his notes to his Indonesian photographs: *What makes Bali outstanding and unique in this confused world is the harmony between the beliefs of the Balinese, their life and their expression. The cosmic harmony of their religious belief to which every act of their life is related; the social structure of the village which is based on cooperation of all the members instead of competition. A wonderfully frugal life in which the entity of the village is absolutely self–sufficient, in which everybody is an artist in the same time as a man working.*

This harmony endured many years of outside influence, Dutch colonization as well as Japanese occupation. Cartier–Bresson's pictures of the trance dancers convey a sense of the enduring tradition that seems outside western experience. His pictures of the independence movement, of the rise of Sukarno, however, are harbingers of the self–inflicted, disharmonizing effects that came as a consequence of entering the post–World War II political–economic world order as a sovereign nation. As an analogy to what Cartier–Bresson accomplished with his camera, Indonesia's decisive moment in history was also an act of forgetting.

Henri Cartier–Bresson

Batubulan villagers in a trance
holding sharp kerises *to their bodies during a* Barong *dance,*
Bali, 1949.

Henri Cartier–Bresson

Woman deep in trance during a Barong *performance,*
Batubulan, Bali, 1949.

Henri Cartier–Bresson

President Sukarno in front of a painting
portraying young Indonesian freedom fighters,
Yogyakarta, 1949.

Henri Cartier-Bresson

Sukarno's inaugural speech at the Istana Negara,
Jakarta, 1949.

Henri Cartier-Bresson

President Sukarno returns to Jakarta,

December 1949.

Henri Cartier-Bresson

Dutch soldiers at Tanjung Priok Harbor preparing
to return to the Netherlands,
January 1950.

Henri Cartier-Bresson

Young Indonesian guerrilla soldiers return from the mountains, near Solo,

Java, 1948.

Woodbury & Page

Gusti Jelantik, the Vice Regent of Buleleng, Bali,
with his daughter and servants,
1865. Albumen print.

Beyond Pictorialism *Photography in Modern Indonesia*

Yudhi Soerjoatmodjo

CONCRETE–AND–GLASS SHOPPING PLAZAS WILL SOON FILL A WIDE EMPTY SPACE NORTH OF JAKARTA, IN A DECAYING AREA KNOWN AS THE SENEN TRIANGLE THAT IS THE LINK TO INDONESIA'S PHOTOGRAPHIC PAST. FEW REMEMBER THE ROWS OF STUDIOS THAT WERE THERE THIRTY YEARS AGO, WITH THEIR TINY WINDOWS LOOKING OUT INTO THE BUSY CHINATOWN. THIS IS WHERE THE *TUKANG POTRET* USED TO LIVE AND WORK. They never called themselves photographers, however; they were simply *tukang*, pictorialists. People visited these studios for a touch of Hollywood glamour, or to recreate the image of respectability of the pre–independence Dutch Indies residents. The *tukang potret* knew that it was not truth that their patrons wanted from their magical camera boxes, but a bit of fantasy and reassurance.

Despite the fact that these shops have now been torn down and that many view cameras were sold to pay for funeral costs, a discussion on the role of photography in Indonesia's modern culture would not be comprehensive without examining the *tukang potret*. The perspectives and attitudes of these pictorialists were derived from the earliest practices of photography in the nineteenth–century colonial Dutch Indies. In 1844, five years after Louis Jacques Mande Daguerre's invention of the process, a European by the name of Adolf Schaefer brought the silver–plate view camera to Batavia. In return for his safe passage, the Dutch government employed his expertise on the daguerreotype. The Dutch saw it as a tool, and, accordingly, one of Schaefer's earliest commissions was to make a photographic inventory of the Hindu–Javanese sculptures in the collection of the Batavia Art and Science Society. Schaefer's plates conveyed the treasures more accurately than any artist's hand–sketch ever could.

The unique qualities of photography were put to good use during the restoration of Borobudur, in Central Java; and by the time it was completed in 1890, the project not only introduced photographers to a wider range of subject matter, but brought many *tukang potret* into the service of the colonial government. These photographers, with the exception of Kassian Céphas all European, were assigned to the task of documenting and mapping every inch of the Buddhist temple, which had been built circa 8 A.D. by the Syailendra king.

In the late 1800s, photographic illustrations began to replace drawings in books, newspapers and brochures in the Netherlands and throughout Europe. The colonial government used photography to display their rich possession to the people back home, and the images brought by the *tukang potret* from the Dutch Indies stirred people's imagination for that distant and exotic land. But their empire was more than just a collection of sculptures, temples and lush paddy fields. In 1890, the colonial policy of *cultuurstelsel,* the forced cultivation of cash crops, was over.

The socialists who soon ascended in the Dutch parliament offered an alternative with their more humane "ethical policy."

In the Dutch Indies, this change translated into a commitment to social welfare—proper education, health and housing—for the "suffering natives." Any form of exploitation—especially the power of the Indonesian Kings over their people—was felt to be sinful. Thereafter, the Law of Decentralization divided the already weakened Mataram Kingdom in Central Java into four rival courts. The other courts suffered as well. The bloody battle of Jagaraga, for example, brought the Balinese royal houses of Karangasem and Buleleng to their knees. Ironically, this was the height of the Dutch power in Indonesia.

One typical image produced around this period is a portrait of Gusti Ngurah Ketut Jelantik, King of Buleleng, accompanied by his young daughter and courtiers. It is clear in this picture that the king still claimed prestige and royalty. His status is confirmed not only in the beautifully woven golden *songket* and sculpted sacred *keris* he wore, but also in the way he rested his foot, with all appropriateness, on the leg of his guard. Despite these trappings, the lens of an unknown Dutch *tukang potret* captured despair in the surprised gaze of Gusti Jelantik. That pain, that look, was multiplied in the countless photographs produced by the *tukang potret* of the colonial service. In Sumatra, where war against the Dutch raged for decades, it took the form of the rotting human flesh of the Aceh warriors. The cameras there also focused on the weary *kape,* the Dutch special commando force that was composed of mercenaries and native soldiers, in their victory pose. It was a war destined never to end, and millions of Dutch riches and lives were wasted in the attempt to crush the *sabil,* the holy war.

Life was less hectic in Java, the seat of the colonial government in the 1880s. The lava–enriched soil, the polite smiles of the Javanese and the gamelan music drifting majestically from inside the royal courts of Yogyakarta and Solo created a pleasant atmosphere. Here, Kassian Céphas, a photographer of Javanese–Dutch descent, was commissioned to document life inside the walls of the *keraton,* the sultan's or king's palace. His camera recorded the court rituals and ceremonies of the Javanese nobilities. Other *tukang potret* followed Céphas' lead into the next decades; it had become the royal courts' turn to be subjected to the colonial inventory machine. Today, these photographs evoke powerful emotions, although for the non–Indonesian it may be easy to dismiss the historical facts and zoom in on the elements of artistic or cultural interest of these beautiful images. The truth is, the photographs documented the painful process of the emergence of modern Indonesia.

By the early twentieth century, it had become clear to the oppressed that there would be no *ratu Adil,* or Savior, to free the Indonesian people from colonial dominance. The sultans and princes had deserted their fate in return for some illusory titles from the colonial government in Batavia. Ironically, the implementation of the Dutch "ethical policy" encouraged the growth of *priayi kecil,* a new class of well–educated and well–bred Javanese who further displaced much of the prestige of the older *keraton* dignitaries. Whatever the nobles were able to preserve within their palace walls was overtaken by the new priorities and agendas of colonialism.

Signs of rapid change are clearly evident, for example, in the photographs of the Mangkoenogoro court, and the portrait of Prince Mangkoenogoro V with his escort of female court dancers that revealed the cloistered world of kings. With these pictures, what had been considered sacred intimacy became common gossip, not only among the Dutch residents in Batavia, but as far away as Europe. The camera, with its eye that dared to stare back at these demigods, broke down the wall that for thousands of years had protected the nobility's mortal soul from the gaze of the ordinary man. The push for modernization did, however, arise from these conflicts and tensions. One of the founding fathers of *Budi Utomo,* the first Javanese intellectual movement, was Mangkoenogoro VII.

The French critic Alain Bergala has said that photography is condemned to miss as much of reality as it captures. It is easy, for example, to be seduced by the apparent mysticism and elegance of the royal courts of Java and Bali, but much more difficult to perceive, and admit, the shock of change not only in the sentimental portrait of the young princess of the *keraton* of Yogyak, but also in Gusti Jelantik's anger. These articulate and often sensitive images from the past do not constitute an insult to Indonesia's history. The Indonesian princes and princesses simply miscalculated their longing for lost power, and the cameras were there to record it. Unfortunately, the royalty also failed to perceive in their own proud portraits the sweeping implications of change.

Currently, the failure in Indonesia to understand the power of images has prevented photography from developing into a living language there. Indonesians are certainly visual people, as can be witnessed from the vast array of paintings, sculptures and carvings they created. However, every art reflects the underlying situation or thought of its period. The Dutch used their photographers' artistry to take inventory of their possessions in the Dutch Indies, and their emphasis was on the exotic and the majestic.

How significant is photography to modern Indonesia? After Indonesia's independence, and with the passing of old values, confusion set in. As some Indonesians tried to redefine themselves, others found solace in nostalgia. Thus, while some *tukang potret* entered the struggle for the "next revolution" by joining the burgeoning press, others peddled dreams. Unfortunately, the Indonesia of the fifties and sixties was more concerned with slogans than with substance. The *tukang potret* who were fluent in the language of photography ignored message in favor of pictorialism and commercial acceptance.

Modern Indonesian photography seems to prefer the grand gesture, a case in point being the publication in recent years of a number of coffee table picture books on Indonesia. Millions of dollars have been spent by people who, by putting Indonesia on the world map, have cashed in on the West's surging interest in exotic lands. During the past five years, countless troops of the world's "greatest" photographers have been commanded to fly over mountains or scuba dive the deepest water of the archipelago in search of mystical, mythical Indonesia. The results have been a pictorialism catering to tourists' fantasies that are not all that far from the imagery offered by the *tukang potret* in Jakarta's old Senen Triangle.

Photography exhibitions, exclusive of the occasional shows organized by international bodies and cultural centers, are virtually non–existent, even in Indonesia's capital city. Magazines often hold "instant" photographic competitions with cars, houses and girls as models, yet hardly any media have opened their pages to indepth photographic essays on issues such as the deforestation of Indonesia's tropical jungle or the growing problems of street urchins in the big cities.

As is clear in this book, there has been a tradition of concerned documentation in Indonesia; a commitment toward life and humanity that is clearly shown in the images of Walter Spies and Henri Cartier–Bresson, for example. Nevertheless, modern Indonesian cameramen have failed to grasp that quality as their own traditions have developed. By failing to move beyond formal documentary and pictorialism, photography is thus sadly left to play an insignificant role in Indonesia's cultural and historical present. By focusing only on exotic images of exotic people and landscapes, modern Indonesian photography continues to be influenced by money and fashion. Furthermore, without liberating themselves from colonialism's projected image, Indonesians cannot discover their true nature. Dreams have turned to yellow dust in the images produced by the *tukang potret,* while millennia of empires are remembered only in beautiful and formal pictures.

FURTHER READING ON PHOTOGRAPHY IN INDONESIA

Boom, Matthie, *150 Fotografie: een keuze uit de collectie van de Rijksdienst Beeldende Kunst.*The Hague: 1989.

von Dewitz, Bodo, and Reinhard Matz, ed., *Silber und Salz—zur Fruhzeit der Photographie in Deuschen Sprachram 1839–1860.* Köln and Heidelberg: 1989.

de Graff, H. J., "Céphas, de Hoffotograaf, 1845–1912,"
Stichting Cultuurgeschedenis van de Nederlanders Overzee, Verslagen en Aanwinsten, 1980–81 (1982), 47–53.

Groeneveld, Anneke. *Toekang Potret: 100 Jaar Fotografie in Nederlands Indie 1839–1939.* Rotterdam: Museum of Ethnology, 1989.

Guillot, Claude, "Un exemple d'assimilation a Java; le photographie Kassian Céphas (1844–1912)," *Archipel 22* (1981), 55–73.

van der Hoop, A. N. J. Th. and Th., "Vergeelde Portretten," *Bijdrage tot de Taal—Land–en Volkenkunde*, vol. 114 (1958), 121–132.

de Loos–Haaxman, *Verlaat Rapport Indie.* The Hague: 1968, 39–42.

Maass, Alfred, *Bei Liebenswurdigen Wilden.* Berlin: 1902.

Moeshart, H. J., "Adolph Schaefer," in I. Th. Leijerzapf, ed., *Geschiedenis van de Nederlandse Fotografie.* Alphen a/d/ Rin: 1986.

Moeshart, H. J., "Daguerreotypes by Adolph Schaefer," *History of Photography,* vol. 9, nr. 3 (1985).

Praamstra, Olf, "Een Indisch Toneelstuk," *Maatstaf,* April 1986, 130–156.

Rouffaer, G. P., "Monumentale Kunst op Java," *De Gids,* vol. 2, 1901, 226–252.

Soerjoatmodjo, Yudhi, "Menjebak Borobudur," *Tempo,* March 31, 1990, 130–156.
See also Céphas, Rico A., "Dari cucu pometret Borobudur," *Tempo,* May 5, 1990 (letter to the editor.)

Stapel, F. W., *Geschiedenis van Nederlandsch Indie,* Amsterdam: 1940.

Volkenkundig Museum Nusantara, *Nias, Tribal Treasures,* Delft: 1990.

Wills, Camfield and Diedre, "Walter Bentley Woodbury,"
The Photographic Journal , vol. 125, no. 12, (December 1985), 551–554; and vol. 126, no. 1, (January 1986), 40–41.